A SCHOOLMASTER OF
THE GREAT CITY

OTHER BOOKS IN THE CLASSICS
IN PROGRESSIVE EDUCATION SERIES

How Kindergarten Came to America:
Friedrich Froebel's Radical Vision
of Early Childhood Education
BERTHA VON MARENHOLTZ-BÜLOW

The New Education:
Progressive Education One Hundred Years Ago Today
SCOTT NEARING

The Public School and the Private Vision:
A Search for America in Education and Literature
MAXINE GREENE

A SCHOOLMASTER
OF THE GREAT CITY

---

*A Progressive Educator's
Pioneering Vision for
Urban Schools*

ANGELO PATRI

THE NEW PRESS

NEW YORK
LONDON

Requests for permission to reproduce selections from this book
should be mailed to: Permissions Department, The New Press, 38 Greene Street,
New York, NY 10013.

Originally published in the United States by The Macmillan Company, 1917
Published in the United States by The New Press, New York, 2007
Distributed by W. W. Norton & Company, Inc., New York

ISBN 978-1-59558-212-6 (pbk)
ISBN 978-1-59558-219-5 (hc)
CIP data available

The New Press was established in 1990 as a not-for-profit alternative to the large,
commercial publishing houses currently dominating the book publishing industry.
The New Press operates in the public interest rather than for private gain, and is
committed to publishing, in innovative ways, works of educational, cultural, and
community value that are often deemed insufficiently profitable.

www.thenewpress.com

Composition by NK Graphics,
a Black Dot Group Company
This book was set in New Caledonia

Printed in Canada

2   4   6   8   10   9   7   5   3   1

Contents

SERIES FOREWORD
Classics in Progressive Education

My first classroom was empty. Not a book, piece of paper, pencil, or stick of chalk was in sight. The principal welcomed me to the school and informed me he had high expectations for each and every student. Crazy. I figured I had to dig into my meager savings and buy pencils, some remaindered typing paper, and discount crayons. Books were out of the question.

It was rough going for my first week of teaching, but during my second, two older female teachers showed up in my classroom after school. It turns out they were watching me and decided I might be a lifer—a lifelong progressive education teacher. They brought me boxes of books, material about the United Federation of Teachers, and most of all, some classics of progressive education. Over coffee after school one day, they informed me that both of them would retire in a year but wanted to keep the tradition of democratic, student-centered education alive. These teachers hoped to keep arts in the schools and they hoped that young teachers like me (I was 23 at the time) would keep the tradition going. But, they emphasized, in order to keep a tradition alive, you had to know its history and read its literature. That's why, in addition to all the specific educational material these teachers brought me, they insisted I read Dewey, Froebel, Freinet, Homer Lane, Makarenko, and many other democratic educators whose work has had major influences on educators throughout the world. Their teaching was concrete and their vision for education was large.

I didn't have a chance to thank these two teachers because

they retired in the middle of my first year of teaching without leaving their names or addresses. But I have honored their commitment to children and to progressive education. This series is meant to show them my appreciation for their unsolicited gifts to me.

This series will reissue important but often hard-to-find works of progressive education which are still very useful to people teaching today. It is essential to connect to tradition, to know that you are not alone trying to fight against authoritarian or corporate education. The goal is to energize teachers through a connection to educators who have struggled for democratic and creative education against the demands of governments, the rigidity of some churches, and the complex lives many students are forced to bear. The books reprinted are for teachers of hope who understand the complexities of struggling for their students and who might need a dose of history, a bit of humor, and lots of new ideas.

—Herbert Kohl
February 2007

Foreword

In the late 1980s I was given a copy of Angelo Patri's *A School-master of the Great City* by Josephine Whitney Duvenick, a life-long progressive educator who was in her mid-nineties at the time. The title sounded archaic to me, and I skimmed it and put it in a bookcase. About five years later I rediscovered it on the shelf and decided to read it. When I was finished reading this wonderful, personal, educational, and inspiring book I resolved to find a way to get it reprinted so that a contemporary audience can share the voice and experience of this exceptional educator. The book, published in 1917, has been out of print for over sixty years, and this series provides an opportunity to make it available once again to a new audience of educators who are still strug-gling with the same urban educational problems.

Angelo Patri was born in 1876 in a small town not far from Naples. His peasant family was desperately poor, and in 1881 they immigrated to the United States, settling in East Harlem, which at that time was known as Little Italy. Tens of thousands of Italian immigrants lived there at the time. There were also thou-sands of East European Jewish immigrants living in the adjoin-ing community to the west in Central Harlem.

Patri's first few years in Italy had a profound influence on his sensibility—in particular, the tradition of storytelling. He de-scribes how much he loved sitting around a fire listening to his father tell tales of the crusades, of local heroes, of adventures and romances that took place years ago in the woods and farms around him. Throughout his educational career, Patri was known for substituting a story for harsh discipline. For him it worked with even the most difficult students.

Once in New York, Patri did not pass through the doors of a school for six years. During that time he learned English on the streets and was taught how to read and write Italian by an uncle. From the time he was seven, he used these skills to write letters for his neighbors. Since almost all of them were nonliterate, they communicated with people back home through this precocious child. Patri says in *Schoolmaster*, "Especially the womenfolk took me off to a corner and asked me to write letters to their friends in Italy. As they told me the story I wrote it down. I thus learned the beat of plain folk's hearts." This sensitivity to the feelings of working people and people who were troubled directed him to teaching and underpinned Patri's educational work. Many years later, when he was principal of Junior High School 45, one of his students, Julius Garfinkel—known more popularly as the actor John Garfield—is purported to have said of Patri, "For reaching into the garbage pail and pulling me out, I owe him everything."

Patri's teaching and administrative career within the New York City public school system stretched from 1897 to 1944— forty-seven years. He was engaged in education beginning with the massive migrations of Italians and Jews to the United States at the start of the twentieth century, through World War I, the progressive movements of the 1920s, the Depression, the beginnings of red-baiting in the late 1930s and early 1940s, and World War II. During that time he authored books for children as well as for educators and parents, wrote newspaper advice columns, became involved in the founding of the Progressive Education Association as one of its few public urban educators, and was one of the central public advocates for progressive, multicultural, and socialist, community-based education. Throughout his life he remained committed to these central tenets, which first emerged from his family and then developed through his classroom experience and studies at Teachers College, Columbia, with, among others, John Dewey.

Patri began teaching in 1897 as a stern disciplinarian facing classes of sixty-five students ranging from eight to fifteen years old. What Patri called "boss discipline" worked for these students. The next year, however, he was given a classroom of "unruly" students—all Italian, Irish, and Jewish. Boss discipline didn't work. The students paid no attention to his efforts. What worked, it turned out, were his stories, his students' stories, and his refocusing the curriculum on life in the community. Through these strategies, he found a passion for learning in his students that transformed the way he taught.

In order to develop a more theoretical understanding of what he had discovered through his everyday practice in the classroom, he went to Teachers College, Columbia, in 1900. At the time it was a center for progressive ideas in education. Over the next years he transformed many of the ideas of progressive education into everyday practice in a complex and often chaotic urban school.

Patri's book moves me so much because I feel he went through at the turn of the last century what I too experienced in the early 1960s and what many of my students are experiencing now. In the book, he tells stories about individual students and families illuminating the ideas of progressive educational thinking with the specific struggles of a caring, active, and creative educator. Patri's commitment to the idea that no child should fail or be humiliated is powerful. For him one of the roles of the teacher is to work like an inventor to find better, more effective ways to reach students. Had I read Patri when I began my educational voyage, I would have been a more grounded and skillful educator.

Schoolmaster of the Great City focuses on the first four decades of Patri's life, with particular emphasis on the five years (1908 to 1913) when he was principal of PS 4 in the Bronx. When he became principal, Patri, arguably the first Italian principal in the history of the New York City public school system, had been teaching for eleven years. He had established himself as an important grassroots voice for progressive education as well as an advocate for community engagement and what's now called multiculturalism. Patri believed in the power of the parents of his students to help him and created one of the first Parents' Associations in the United States. As an immigrant, he believed it was possible and desirable to become an English-speaking American and still preserve his relationship to Italian language and culture. He generalized this to the children he worked with and respected the cultures of all of his students while helping them acclimatize as participating citizens in a democratic America. His goal of balancing home culture with American culture seemed to have succeeded admirably in his school and comes across very strongly through many of the stories in *Schoolmaster*.

As Patri wrote,

> No matter who the people are, they need the school as a humanizing force, so that they may feel the common interest, revive their visions, see the fulfillment of their dreams in terms of their children, so that they may be made young once more. Americanize the foreigner, nay, through the child let us fulfill our destiny and Americanize America (page 140).

According to James M. Wallace, who has written the authoritative book on Patri*, Patri

> meant [by the above quote to] democratize America and make its advantages available to all in an atmosphere of mutual respect. For urban educators in particular, this presented an ethical and pragmatic imperative to actively involve parents and communities in the life of the school and the school in the life of the city.

Patri helped his teachers develop their "personal interests toward special teaching in art, athletics, dancing, festivals, music,

---

* *The Promise of Progressivism: Angelo Patri and Urban Education* (New York: Peter Lang, 2006).

nature study, and storytelling. . . ." Teachers made room in the curriculum for "the folktales of the children's ancestors." Patri, his staff, and neighborhood leaders helped start a settlement house with a playground. Parents "encouraged to visit the school to see their children at work or in entertainments . . . formed the habit of attending conferences concerning school problems, and finally organized a Parents' Association."

Patri's "suggestions for school betterment" included smaller classes, a curriculum related to real life, better teacher training, and "more intimate contact with the people . . . and the school cooperating with the entire neighborhood."

Patri was not just interested in parents, community, and culture but pedagogy as well. *Schoolmaster* shows him shaping the curriculum, developing his teachers, and transforming the physical environment of the school and the classroom. He wrote that "Playrooms and games, animals and plants, wood and nails must take their place side by side with books and words" (page 128). And if this wasn't enough he created a savings bank for students and worked with other members of the community to break up the gangs that terrorized the school's neighborhood. One wonders if he would have been able to achieve all of this had he not been childless and felt so deeply that the students were his children.

According to Patri,

> The school must open its doors. It must reach out and spread itself, and come into direct contact with all its people. Each day the power of the school must be felt in some corner of the school district. It must work so that everybody sees its work and daily appraises that work (page 136).

Toward the end of the book, Patri summarizes what he feels is necessary for school reform. His extended list is worth reading and studying now that we are still fumbling our way toward educating the children of the great cities of the United States.

Here is a summary of that list, which he created in 1917:

To begin with, better schools ... for the youngest children ... We must spend more money on elementary education if the money we now spend on higher education is to bring forth results that are commensurate with our national needs. .... We must keep the three R's, but they must change with the changing social needs. .... Have we the courage to change our class education into democratic education? ...

The second thing to do is to train the teacher differently. .... Can the higher training include the direction of young children in club life, the participation in the work of settlements, the study of the home and street life? Should the training school period include work in the hospital for children, so that the teacher may actually learn what the physical needs of the children are, and where to go for help? ...

Third, we must break the deadening influence of a too strongly centralized system; we must individualize the schools rather than mass them. .... What the school system needs to understand is that its strength lies, not in the strength of the central organization, but in the strength of the individual school, not in making one school like another, but in making each school a distinct unit. ...

Fourth, we must change the notion that the school is a cloistered institution, by breaking down its walls and having it come into direct contact with people. .... It must use the factory, the stores, the neighboring parks, the museums, not incidentally but fully and with deliberation. ...

Fifth, we must change our attitude toward the child. .... I feel that the attitude toward the school and the child is the ultimate attitude by which America is to be judged. Indeed, the distinctive contribution America is to make to the world's progress is not political, economical, religious, but educational—the child our national strength, the school as the medium through which the adult is to be remade (pages 126–139).

In 1929 Patri moved from PS 4 to Junior High School 45 in the Bronx and stayed there until he retired in 1944. He remained a progressive throughout all the changes, the back-to-the-basics movements, the obsessive emphasis on the "Three R's," the purges of progressives during the late thirties and early forties. He was a steady, persistent, and much-loved force for humane education, writing newspaper columns with advice to parents, authoring children's and adult books—all the while keeping PS 45 a creative, vibrant school. He never stopped telling stories, caring for his students and their parents, and struggling with the bureaucracy to keep his work authentic and free of educational fads and structured programs that he knew would inhibit the growth and creativity of his teachers and students.

Schoolmaster of the Great City should enter the teacher education curriculum. It should be read by practicing teachers and administrators and by anyone who cares about nurturing children rather than torturing them with high-stakes testing, teacher-proof curricula, zero-tolerance discipline, and punitive evaluations. It is a breath of fresh air in a polluted educational environment.

—Herbert Kohl
June 2007

A SCHOOLMASTER OF
THE GREAT CITY

1

The Background

I remember sitting with the family and the neighbors' families about the fireplace, while Father, night after night, told us stories of the Knights of the Crusades or recounted the glories of the heroes of proud Italy.

How he could tell a story! His voice was strong, and soft, and soothing, and he had just sufficient power of exaggeration to increase the attractiveness of the tale. We could see the soldiers he told us about pass before us in all their struggles and sorrows and triumphs. Back and forth he marched them into Asia Minor, across Sicily, and into the castles of France, Germany, and England. We listened eagerly and came back each night ready to be thrilled and inspired again by the spirit of the good and the great.

Then came the journey over the sea, and the family with the neighbors' families were part of the life of New York. We were Little Italy.

I was eleven before I went to a city school. All the English I knew had been learned in the street. I knew Italian. From the time I was seven I had written letters for the neighbors. Especially the womenfolk took me off to a corner and asked me to write letters to their friends in Italy. As they told me the story I wrote it down. I thus learned the beat of plain folks' hearts.

My uncle from whom I had learned Italian went back to Italy and I was left without a teacher, so one day I attached myself to a playmate and went to school; an "American" school. I gave my name and my age and was told to sit in a long row of benches with some sixty other children. The teacher stood at the blackboard and wrote "March 5, 1887." We all read it after her; chanting the singsong with the teacher. Each morning we did the same thing, that is, repeated lessons after the teacher. That first day and the second day were alike, and so were the years that followed. "If one yard of goods cost three cents how much will twenty-five yards cost?" If one yard costs three cents then twenty-five yards will cost twenty-five times three cents or seventy-five cents. The explanation could not vary or it might not be true or logical.

But there was one thing that was impressed more strongly than this routine. I had always been a sickly, thin, pale-faced child. I did not like to sit still. I wanted to play, to talk, to move about. But if I did any of these things, I was kept after school as a punishment. This would not do. I had to get out of the room and frequently I endured agonies because the teacher would not permit me to leave the room whenever I wanted to. Many times I went home sick and lay abed.

Soon I discovered that boys who sat quietly, looked straight ahead and folded their arms behind their backs, and even refused to talk to their neighbors, were allowed the special privilege of leaving the room for one minute, not longer. So I sat still, very still, for hours and hours so that I might have the one minute. Throughout my whole school life this picture remains uppermost. I sat still, repeated words, and then obtained my minute allowance.

For ten years I did this, and because I learned words I was able to go from the first year of school through the last year of college. My illness and the school discipline had helped after all. They had made my school life shorter by several years than it otherwise might have been.

The colony life of the city's immigrants is an attempt to continue the village traditions of the mother country. In our neighborhood there were hundreds of families that had come from the same part of Italy. On summer nights they gathered in groups on the sidewalks, the stoops, the courtyards, and talked and sang and dreamed. In winter the men and boys built Roman arches out of the snow.

But gradually the families grew in size. The neighborhood became congested. A few families moved away. Ours was one of them. We began to be a part of the new mass instead of the old. The city with its tremendous machinery, its many demands, its constant calling, calling, began to take hold. What had been intimate, quaint, beautiful, ceased to appeal.

I went to school, Father went to work, Mother looked after the house. When evening came, instead of sitting about the fire, talking and reliving the day, we sat, each in his own corner. One nursed his tired bones, another prepared his lessons for the morrow. The demands of the school devoured me; the work world exhausted my father. The long evenings of close contact with my home people were becoming rare. I was slipping away from my home; home was slipping away from me.

Yet my father knew what he was about. While the fathers of most of the boys about me were putting their money into business or into their houses, mine put his strength, his love, his money, his comforts into making me better than himself. The spirit of the crusaders should live again in his son. He wanted me to become a priest: I wanted to become a doctor.

During all the years that he worked for me, I worked for myself. While his hopes were centered in the family, mine were extending beyond it. I worked late into the nights, living a life of which my father was not a part. This living by myself tended to make me forget, indeed to undervalue, the worth of my people. I was ashamed sometimes because my folk did not look or talk like Americans.

When most depressed by the feeling of living crudely and poorly, I would go out to see my father at work. I would see him high up on a scaffold a hundred feet in the air and my head would get dizzy and my heart would rise to my throat. Then I would think of him once more as the poet storyteller with the strong, soothing voice and the far-off-visioned eye, and the poet in his soul would link itself to mine, and would see why on two-dollar-a-day wages he sent me to college.

Proud of his strength I would strengthen my moral fiber and respond to his dream. Yet not as he dreamed, for when he fell fifty feet down a ladder and was ill for a whole year I went to work at teaching.

II

The principal under whom I did my first teaching was one with whom I had studied as a pupil in the grades. He was opening a new school and welcomed me cordially. Leading me to a classroom, he opened the door and pushed me in, saying, "This is your class." Then he vanished.

There were sixty-six children in that room. Their ages ran from eight to fifteen. They had been sitting there daily annoying the substitutes who were sent to the room and driving them out of school. The cordial reception I had been given by the principal held more of relief for himself than of kindness for me.

That first day passed. The last few straggling boys filed out an hour or so after school hours. One of the biggest boys, whom I had detained for disorder, stopped long enough on his way out to ask. "Coming back tomorrow?"

"Yes, of course I am coming back. Why do you ask?"

"Well, some of them come one day and some come two days. Tomorrow will be two days."

This boy did not know me. My one strong point was discipline. I knew little of subject matter, pedagogy, or psychology, except a number of words that had never become part of me. I had one notion that was strong—discipline. That was the idea. Had I not been kept after hours to study my lessons, slapped for asking my neighbor for a pencil, made to kneel for hours for absenting my-self from school, for defending my rights to the teacher? Had I not been marked, rated, percented all the ten years of my life in school?

Discipline then was the basic idea in teaching. You made

pupils do what you wanted; you must be the master. Memory, and those who ought to have known, preached discipline. It was the standard for judging my work as a teacher. My continuance in the profession depended upon discipline.

At least there was no conflict of aim. Since discipline was the thing, I would discipline, and I did. I oppressed; I went to the homes; I sent registered letters. I followed up each infraction of rules relentlessly. There was no getting away from me. I was making sure that the children were punished for their misdeeds.

I followed the truants into their homes because I wanted relief from a principal who sent me a note every time my attendance fell below a certain percent. I visited the parents to complain of the work the children were doing, because the principal said I must hold their noses to the grindstone.

I seemed to say to the children, in the words of Edmond Holmes, "You are to model yourself, or rather I will model you, on me. What I do, you are to learn to do. What I think, you are to learn to think. What I believe, you are to learn to believe. What I admire, you are to learn to admire. What I aim at, you are to learn to aim at. What I am, you are to learn to be."

At the end of my first month I was an assured success. My discipline of the class and the promptness with which I followed up the absentees gained recognition. I was promoted from teaching a fourth-year class to a fifth-year class. The new class was made for me especially because I was efficient. It was composed of all the children that the other teachers in approximate grades did not want. They were fifty misfits.

The room given me was the corner of an assembly room, shut in by rolling doors. The benches were long affairs and were not screwed to the floor. A writing lesson could be conducted only when the desk which formed part of the seat in front was turned up, so that it became the desk for the seat behind. No hour went by but some boy or girl of the fifty managed to upset one of the desks; then the papers would scatter, and the ink would flow on the new floor. Some of the children would laugh; others would howl, and my best friend in the front seat would stand on his head. This, he said, was in preparation for the time when he was to become a tumbler at the circus. Judging from the hardness of the bumps his head got he was undergoing rather severe training.

Discipline—my favorite word—why, discipline was failing, failing terribly. If I kept the children after hours they would not come to school the next day until they had made up the time that I had taken from them. If I went to their parents, the parents simply said they could not help it; they knew that these were bad children. They seemed to feel sorry for this mere slip of a boy who used up his afternoons and evenings calling upon them.

Discipline, discipline! It was no use. I tried to say again, "You are to model yourself, or rather I will model you, on me. What I do you are to learn to do, etc." But somehow the words would not come. Discipline, my great stronghold, had failed for I had come into contact with those who defied discipline.

What was I to do? I began to tell over again the stories I faintly remembered having heard in the days when father sat and talked and we listened, not daring to move lest we lose a syllable of what he said. I told them about my own childhood in the mountains of Italy, about midnight expeditions when we loaded the mules with provisions and carried food to our friends, the last of the Bourbon adherents. I told them about a wolf that attacked the sheep at night until my father seized and killed it bare-handed.

When I related these stories they listened. They hardly breathed. Each day I would end so that more could be expected. Then I began to bargain with them, trading what they liked for what the schools said they should have. I bribed them with promises of more stories to come if they would be "good" and do the work assigned.

The struggle was between the child and the teacher, and the struggle was over the facts of the curriculum—the children refusing to learn and the teacher insisting that they must. But discipline was restored, and victory won, by bargaining.

Woe to the boy or girl who transgressed and thus prevented the telling of the story. No arithmetic, no story! No silence, no story! The children from other classes asked to be changed. They, too, wanted stories. I had them by the hundreds, for as soon as I had caught the interest of the children the stories of adventure gave place to the old hero tales.

Discipline once more was my watchword.

Then a new trouble arose. I had been teaching a year when "Methods" became the school watchword, and everybody set about learning how to teach arithmetic, spelling, history, and geography. Each teacher had his own methods and supervisors going from one room to another were puzzled by the variety.

The principal restored order out of chaos. A method book was written. Every subject was treated and the steps of procedure in each were carefully marked out. A program of the day's work was prescribed and we were expected to follow the stated order. Inspection by the principal and other supervisors was based on these.

I heard the teachers talk of these things as impositions. When I failed to follow directions I was severely criticized. I began asking the reason for it all.

Why should I teach history in the prescribed way?

"Class, open books to page 37. Study the first paragraph."

Two minutes later.

"Close books. Tell me what you learned."

In such instruction there was no stopping, no questioning, no valuation: nothing but deadly, mechanical grind. Every teacher and every class had to do these things in just this way.

The spelling routine was worst. Twenty new words were to be assigned each day for study. The words had to be difficult, too, for through them the children were to train their memories— their minds, as the principal put it. The next day at a signal the children wrote the twenty words in the order in which they had been assigned, from memory, if they could. Papers were exchanged and the children were asked to correct them. If a child failed to discover an error it was a point against him. The names of those who "missed" were written on the board with a check for each mistake. The pupils who failed had to remain after hours and repeat the list from memory, accurately as to its spelling and sequence.

This was a fixed procedure which no teacher dared modify because the supervisor came around and questioned the children as to the accuracy of the records on the boards.

Instead of protesting, the teacher set about acquiring devices which would give the desired results with the minimum of effort on the part of the teacher and pupils. It was no longer a question of teaching. It was simply a question of getting the better of the supervisor.

My method was simple and efficacious. There was no place where I could get twenty new words with so little expenditure of time and effort as in the dictionary. The dictionary arrangement offered a valuable aid in itself. I selected two a's, two b's, etc., until I had the desired twenty.

The advantages of this scheme were apparent to the children. They could more easily remember and check up their list when it was based upon alphabetical arrangement. The percentage of my returns then became high, and the mental strain on the class and teacher was reduced to the minimum.

Still the question arose in my mind—"Why must I do this sort of thing?"

Another year passed before I realized that my fellow teachers were talking about Education, the Science of Education and its principles. It appeared that in the universities were men who could teach a man why he taught and how to do it. There was one thing I had learned and that was the insufficiency of my equipment as a teacher. Discipline, boss standard, was nerve taxing and not altogether productive.

III

After two years of teaching I found myself nowhere, and was depressed. I questioned the value of my services to the children. The work I did was not its own criticism but was judged by someone else whose standard seemed to be capricious, depending upon his humor and my relation to him. I felt the need of new ideas and convictions, and I decided to go to the university to see what those who were supposed to know had to tell.

I wondered if my return to college with the deliberate purpose of learning what I wanted definitely to know, would prove profitable.

Toward the close of the year's work I summed it up. First one institution and then another! From this professor, and a little later from that, came words, words, words. They were all so far away, so ineffectual, so dead. I was disheartened.

The next year, however, I came upon the thing I needed. This was a course with Dr. McMurry and the textbook used as a basis of discussion was Dewey's essay on "Ethical Principles."

Here were strange and new words to use in relation to teaching. Conduct was the way people behaved, and it had little to do with learning, as such. But conduct, not ability to recite lessons, was the real test of learning and the sign of culture.

Conduct furnished the key as to whether the child had real social interests and intelligence and power. Conduct meant action, whereas school meant passivity. Conduct meant individual freedom and not blind adherence to formulated dogma. The knowledge gained had to be used immediately and the worth of the knowledge judged by its fitness to the immediate needs of the child.

The greatest fallacy of child education was the "training-for-the-future" idea. Training for the future meant dying for the present.

Conduct said the child was a being constantly active, rarely silent, never a purely parrot-like creature. Conduct said the teacher must keep his hands off; he must watch and guide; he could not force; he could not drive. He could put the problems but the children themselves must solve them.

The disciplinary habit was a matter of action on the part of the children rather than one of silent obedience; judgment was a matter of applied knowledge and not word juggling.

Social sympathy was the result of close contact, mutual help, common work, common play, judicious leadership. Laughing, talking, dreaming even, were part of school life, the give-and-take of the group. Conduct always carried the idea of someone else; no isolation, no selfishness.

Then the whole system of marking and punishment and rewards was wrong. It was putting the child on the lowest plane possible. It was preventing him from working in response to an ideal.

I realized then that the child must move and not sit still: that he must make mistakes and not merely repeat perfect forms: that he must be himself and not a miniature reproduction of the teacher. The sacredness of the child's individuality must be the moving passion of the teacher.

These things I learned from my masters. It was a wholesome reaction against my disciplinary idea, and a healthy soul-giving impetus to my daily teaching.

I had come in contact with the personality of a great teacher, fearless, candid, and keen, with nothing dogmatic in his nature. Under this leadership I came in touch with vital ideas and I began to work, not in the spirit of passive obedience, but in one of mental emancipation.

There was a new pleasure and much more freedom in my teaching. I went back to the children ready to challenge their intelligence, keen to see them grapple and solve problems set for them, eager to watch them carry into their daily lives the ideas of the school.

I looked back into my own experiences, analyzed them, built them up, and through them interpreted the struggles of the children before me. The God of Discipline was replaced by the God of Watchfulness.

I tried to carry over into classroom practice the results of what I had learned. I tried to teach in the light of the saner point of view. My supervisors objected to the variations I was trying to introduce into the teaching of history, spelling, and the rest.

"You'll find those things may be all right in theory but they will not do in practice," they said. But I refused to compromise, to yield to beliefs merely because I was told to do so or because others about me yielded to beliefs and policies.

Just when the feeling came upon me that I was really beginning to enter into the secret of child training the principal came to me and said, "You are wasting your time. You are wasting the children's time. You are totally unfit for this work. If I had a son he should not be put in your class."

His idea was that, unless you ground children down and made them do as you wanted them to, they would have no fear and respect for you. It was the master and the slave idea. When the teacher rebelled the scourge of sarcasm was relentless.

There were times when I felt that he would have been pleased to have lowered my "ratings" to the point where I would have been compelled to retire from the profession, yet he refrained because he, too, was compromising with himself.

When I changed from his educational philosophy to mine, his comment was, "Why is it you will not do as I tell you?"

What he did not know was that if he had treated me kindly and asked for cooperation, allowed me some form of self-expression, he would have had a wealth of enthusiasm to call upon.

Self-respect compelled me to change schools, and I went away, every fiber of my being indignant at his oppression.

IV

The next principal I found lived the doctrine, "I serve children."

Here was a man who actually loved schoolchildren; who enjoyed coming into personal contact with them in the classroom, the yards, the streets, and their occupations. He helped clothe the poor children and feed them, washed the dirty faces when he found them, and all with the utmost kindliness and in the belief that such service was a wonderful privilege that had been granted him. All about him was the radiance and glow of progress.

He always told this story with sadness as one of the incidents of his school life. A boy had been brought to him for habitual lateness and without stopping to question him he berated him for his laziness while the child stood silent and patient. When the principal awoke to the situation he asked, "Why were you late, anyway?"

The boy replied that he had to work till three o'clock each morning in order to help the family. The principal apologized and made the boy feel that he understood and sympathized with his struggles.

So he was with the teachers, and with me.

To each of us he seemed to say, "You are tired, brother, come to me and let me hold your quivering hands in my strong, steady ones. Come to me and let me stroke your hot, tired eyes with my cool fingers. I know what makes you tired for I, too, have been tired and worn out.

"Sometimes even now, I get tired when I forget the bigness of things I want to do. Those faces that you see in the classroom are not set against you, my brother. They are set against the things that bind you and prevent your mind from mingling freely with others.

"You must not think too much of arithmetic, and rules and dates and examinations, for these are not teaching; the children don't grow because of them. They grow because of their contact with you, the best that you know and feel.

"Come with me to the open country and let us live together for awhile. There we will be silent and look into the hearts of children as we do into the heart of nature.

"When we come back the school will be as a new world and you will work with the earnestness of a discoverer patiently awaiting revelations."

The thought of him always makes me feel strong and fresh as a boy who runs shouting through the cool air of a spring morning. I stretch my arms and open wide my eyes and shout the faith that he gave me.

Promotion came and I found myself in another school. There was little of special interest in my experience in this place. Placed in charge of a graduating class, I was supposed to teach science to the boys of the seventh and eighth grades. The only way I could do this was to carry whatever apparatus I needed from room to room. Batteries, tubes, jars, pails, water, gas burners followed me about. As I passed down the stairs and through the halls I looked like a small moving van. In this departmental system the teacher moved, not the children, because the movement of the children would cause too much noise, too much confusion. School was the place for silence!

At the end of two months I moved again. This time it was a graduating class in a school on the lower west side of the city. The building was more than fifty years old. It fitted well with the general neighborhood picture. It was all run down. There was a miscellaneous sort of population, a mixture of races and color. The boys lived along the docks, in the rear of factory yards where the men found employment.

The first morning, when I announced to the principal that I was a new teacher, he looked at me doubtfully and said, "Why, this won't do, you don't want to come here. You are only a boy. You are not old enough nor strong enough! The boys in that corner room broke the teacher's eyeglasses and he was a bigger man than you are. They threw the inkwells and the books out of the window. You don't want to come here."

When I saw the assembly a few minutes later I agreed with him. I did not want to be there.

I sat on the platform while the principal conducted the exercises. There was scarcely a child in the room who was not either talking or chewing gum, or slouching in his seat. There was a spirit of unrest throughout the monotonous assembly. There was nothing about the general exercises that could offer the slightest inspiration to either children or teacher. Two or three of the men walked up and down the room eyeing the boys, and the women, each at her place, had their eyes riveted on their classes.

Yet, in spite of all this close supervision, the children were not behaving as if they were happy or as if they liked school. At the end of fifteen minutes they were sent to their rooms and the work of the day began. What work that was no one could appreciate unless he had gone through the halls of the building and felt the struggle that was going on in each room. The very walls seemed to speak of tension and battle.

The antagonism between the children and teachers was far stronger than I had ever seen it before. The antagonism between the school and the neighborhood was intense. Both came from mutual distrust founded on mutual misunderstanding. The children were afraid of the teachers, and the teachers feared the children.

The neighborhood was a place from which the teacher escaped, and into which the children burrowed. One never knew as he went through the streets what missile or epithet might greet him. One or the other was certain.

I do not remember a period in my life when I was more silent and soberminded than during the first six months of my career in this school. Day in and day out I sat quietly, scarcely saying an unnecessary word and by gestures rather than speech indicating to the children what I wanted done.

I went through the building silent, rarely speaking. I looked out upon the streets, silent. I visited the shops and listened to the talk of the fathers. I visited some of the homes. Here, too, I talked little, trying to get people to talk to me.

The school was failing. I was failing and my whole mind was concentrated upon finding the cause and the remedy.

After school hours I would stare out of the windows and look out upon the strange mixture of people with their prejudices, their sensitiveness, and their shiftlessness, and ponder upon the gulf between them and me.

There was no attempt on the part of the school to understand the problem and to direct the lives of the pupils. In fact, teaching the curriculum was the routine business of the day—no more. There was apparently little affection for the children, and no interest in the parents as co-workers in their education.

When the principal assigned the assembly exercises and the discipline of the school to me, I was glad. I had learned to believe in children. I had begun to analyze my own childhood more carefully. Here was an opportunity to test my knowledge in a larger way than the classroom offered.

I began by telling the boys what a fine assembly was like in other schools. Once more I resorted to stories. They never failed. Father had done his share nobly. The big restless crowd settled down and listened. As each day went by, cautiously I put the problem of school discipline before them and they responded by taking over much of the responsibility for it themselves. A sort of council was held in my room each week at which the problems of the school were discussed. From fifty to one hundred of the most responsible boys in the school attended and as there were only about twelve hundred in all, the representatives were fairly adequate to the need.

This experience helped me wonderfully. Through it I gained increased confidence in the children, in the power of the school, in myself.

2

In the School

I

Now came my appointment as principal. I stretched my arms and said, "Free at last, my own master! I am limited only by my own vision."

I entered the new school, "My school," as I proudly called it. There it was, a big, massive structure towering like a fortress above the elevated lines, fronting a large public park, the airy rooms full of sunshine.

It did not look out into the backyards of tenements. No smell of leaking gas stoves came in through the open windows. In other days, if I gazed out of a school window I looked into the homes of the neighbors—squalid, noisy homes they were. Whenever there was a quarrel, the loud shrieks and the bad language broke in upon the classroom recitation, and made the children blush and break into nervous laughter. They were ashamed of their parents and their neighborhood.

This new school of mine seemed altogether different. I looked out of my office window at the trees on the hill beyond and watched them sway in the wind, like the restless backs of many elephants. I saw the open spaces, the sunlight, the park, and I rejoiced. These, I knew, were the teacher's best friends.

The day after my installation I went to my office ready to begin on "my school" and carry it up to the heights of power and efficiency. "My school" should come into its own. I do not remember now whether I intended to accomplish this in a day or a month, or a year, for as I sat thinking about it the half-past-eight gong rang sharply, insistently. It brought me up standing in the office door. I heard bell after bell beginning in the first room and follow in order from floor to floor, shrill out its call, cease, pass on its message to its neighbor in the next classroom to pass it along to the next, like a chain of energy linking up the classrooms for the day's work. I had never heard anything quite like that before.

Then came the measured rhythm of many feet. From six entrances the children surged through the halls and into their classrooms. I had a blurred impression of sound, and color and motion and many, many children and teachers all going swiftly by. I saw no individual faces, no distinct forms, just the great mass surging past. Stunned and bewildered, I stood where I was until I realized that a great silence had settled over the building. The big school had begun its day's work and begun it without me.

I sat down at my desk because I didn't know what else to do. The clerk came in with the mail. The former principal who was still in the building with the fifteen hundred children he was to take to the new school came in to arrange some details of administration. With him I went over the number of classes in the school, the teachers who were to go and stay, the district lines, and the number of children to be transferred in and out. This done, he walked out of the office.

I was about to gather myself together and take hold of "my school," and then the gong rang again. I heard doors roll, bells trill, sharp commands, rhythmic footsteps, and the great surge of sound and color and motion passed me again, children going in, children going out. They moved in classes, eyes front, hats off. A mass of children coming in to take the places of the mass that was going out. There was no time lost, just a tramp, tramp, a roll of a door, as it opened, a click as it shut, and then silence as before.

The next day was the same—and the next! I had not taken hold. I left the office and walked through the school, corridors, classrooms, and playgrounds listening and watching, trying to get an idea here and there.

I passed the open door of a classroom and saw a teacher smiling down at a little boy and all the other little boys smiling sympathetically at both. I was glad and walked toward the teacher. Instantly the smile disappeared, her body grew tense, the little boy sat down, and all the other little boys sat up stiff and straight and put their hands behind them.

I tried to say something pleasant but I saw they were afraid of me and I went away.

I went into another room and the teacher was intent upon a little book she was marking, and at the same time telling a boy that she hoped he'd learn something about grammar before he died, but she doubted it.

Without lifting her eyes and so missing seeing me, she said, "Walter, analyze 'Come here.'"

A boy whose thoughts were a long way off jumped up and said—"Simple declarative, Come is the subject—here is the predicate verb," and sat down.

The class laughed heartily and the teacher said as she marked his failure, "Fine—But you forgot something—Come is the subject, here is the predicate, the period is the object."

Everybody laughed. Walter shook himself and analyzed the sentence correctly. Then they realized my presence and froze over. The teacher apologized for not having noticed my entrance, saying she thought it was one of the boys, and asking me to be seated, but I saw she was uncomfortable and I left.

A teacher brought me a disciplinary case. Before she could tell me the trouble she burst into tears. When I tried to tell her there was nothing to cry about she but cried the harder.

Was she afraid of the new principal? Why should she be afraid of him? Yet the scene was somewhat familiar. Oh, I remembered— "You are wasting your time. You are wasting the children's time. You are totally unfit for this work. If I had a son he should not be in your class."

Was that it?

This was bad. The teachers did not want me in the classrooms. They cried when they came to the office.

I'd make friends with the children. But I could not get at them. They were in classes in the rooms—in masses in the yards and corridors. Only the occasional bad one stood out as an individual with whom I could come in personal contact.

"My Dream School" was not so easy.

I thought a great deal about the situation. I know now that in those first days I interpreted the school through my fingertips and eyes and ears rather than through my intellect. I saw and heard the disorderly boy. I ached physically and mentally over the weak teacher; I saw every mistake she made, I heard every faulty intonation of her voice and felt a sense of personal injury. Why was she like that? Why couldn't she be big and fine? And the strong teacher! Why weren't they all like that? That was the way I wanted them. They must all measure up to the best. I rather felt than saw the peaks and hollows.

But in this restless, uncertain sea of motion, noise, color and gongs; of constant going upstairs and downstairs, one learned to "go slow" and watch and wait for his opportunity.

In my discouragement I told an older principal about my efforts and failures.

"What do you mean?" he said in a puzzled fashion. "I don't understand you."

"I've tried to have the teachers and children feel that I'm their friend, that I'm eager to help them, but I don't seem to be able to get them to speak or act freely in my presence. They are afraid of me!"

"Afraid of you? Of course they are and they ought to be. The teachers and children are all right. You'll find them well trained. They will do your bidding without question. Take my advice if you want any peace of mind and keep them under your thumb."

These were not the exact words that had disheartened me years before, but the idea was the same, and I remembered and understood. There was little danger of forgetting; I came upon this blind obedience repeatedly. Obedience, the loyal obedience that was school tradition.

"Let's try to have the children come to school fresh and clean," said I one day to a group of teachers. "Praise those who come in clean blouses and with well-brushed hair."

Shortly after this a mother came in to see me. She laid a little package on my desk.

"Please, I bring you back this shirt."

Startled, I echoed, "Shirt? What shirt?"

"This shirt that the teacher gave my Jonas."

"Tell me about it," I said.

"The teacher said if they were good and sat up tall so that they got 'A' from the Lady Principal she would give them a blouse. Jonas told me and I told him he should try hard and get a blouse. So he did. He tried and tried and got one. But this blouse I don't like. Never I put a thin blouse on Jonas in February—only in April. I want you should take this back and give him a flannel one—a red one he likes."

Here she pulled the wrapping off a pretty little blue and white cotton blouse, and beamingly presented it to me.

Turning over her story in my mind I remembered she had said the "Lady Principal." I went in search of my assistant and, handing her the blouse, I said, "Do you know anything about that?"

"No, but maybe I would understand if you told me how you came by it."

I told her and she chuckled.

"Surely that's Miss North. You said to get the children to come in clean blouses so she talked to them daily and when I visited the room she showed me the boys I was to commend for neat appearance and encourage for their efforts to clean up."

"Let's go in and see the teacher," I suggested, still in the dark.

As we entered, each little boy sat in the middle of his tiny bench; each held a primer carefully covered in brown paper with a red-edged name-label precisely fixed in the center of the front cover; each wore a light-colored wash blouse (I counted seven of the same sort as the one on my desk).

The sunshine came in through the windows and made little rainbows dance above the aquarium, where the fishes looked as if they'd just been polished and put in their places.

"How fine you look," said the Lady Principal.

"Yes, we're all dressed for school. Do you think we can have A today?" asked the smiling teacher.

"I surely do. They're the cleanest boys in town."

"How do you manage about Jonas?" I asked.

"He came without his new blouse and I had an extra one, so I just slipped it over his other one so they'd all be alike. I'll take it off when he goes out and keep it for him."

The teacher had done her level best to carry out the principal's wishes. If the children would not wear clean blouses she would go out and buy them herself. If Jonas left his at home she would give him an extra one. At all events the principal must be obeyed and the class get an "A" rating.

"The teachers and children are all right. You'll find them well trained. They will do your bidding without question."

II

I could not accept that point of view. When the other principal and the group of fifteen hundred children with their teachers went to the new building I said to myself, "Now I can do it. We'll have more room, we'll have fewer children to a teacher, I can get closer to them all."

What a relief from the hurry, the mass movement. Twenty-five hundred children in place of four thousand. The school seemed half empty. School hours were again normal, five hours a day, each teacher in her own room, no hurry to get out so that the next class might come in. Nine o'clock to three and as long after three as the teachers cared to stay. There was plenty of room to work and plenty of opportunity for the teachers to meet and plan and develop.

I called the teachers together and tried to tell them what I believed a good school meant in terms of children and teachers. I tried to make them feel that I was going to take my share of every hard problem in the school day. The bad child, the slow one, the dirty one, were my responsibility as well as the teacher's, and I wanted to help each teacher with each one of her difficulties. I told them of the finer things I had seen about the school and asked for more and more of them until the whole school should become a fine place for children and teachers to live in.

The first response to my offer of help was an appeal from a teacher to discipline a boy.

The teacher came to the office before the work of the day had begun. She entered nervously and stood before me like a prisoner awaiting sentence.

Haltingly she began, "You said I could come to you with a bad boy. Here he is, I can't do anything with him. He's awful."

Then the tears came. I took the boy out of the office and waited long enough to give the teacher a chance to recover.

"Now tell me about it."

"He's a very bad boy. I've had him now a term and a half almost. He won't work and he won't let anybody else work. I've kept him in every day until five o'clock but it does no good. He swears in the classroom and yesterday he threatened to hit me. He's an orphan. He's been in the Protectory and he's on parole now. If he goes on I'll be home sick and it's too bad!" Here she almost cried again.

"Never mind now, I'm glad you brought him to me. He won't give you any more trouble. But tell me—Why did you stand this so long? Why didn't you refer him to the office long ago?"

She hesitated for a minute then said, "I was afraid it would be counted against my record and I'm up for my permanent license."

"Well, it won't count against you and I think this particular boy won't bother you again."

Smiling faintly, she thanked me and went to her room, but I noticed it was weeks before the worried expression left her face and she could smile without effort.

In every class there is one, at least one, so-called "bad child." He comes to the classroom, his brain teeming with the experiences of street life. He lives at top speed during the hours that he is not in school. He is master in the street and in the home, and he would be master in the school. He looks at his classmates with sophisticated scorn and at his teacher with open contempt. The whole machinery of the classroom must stop while he holds the center of the stage. The teacher struggles desperately to hold the class. From the moment the first recitation bell rings in the morning until the last pupil closes the door behind him at night she must strive by every ruse known to the teacher to keep the bad child under while she teaches the good children. The strain is terrible and out of all proportion. But why doesn't the teacher send the child out of the room and continue the work in peace? Why should a whole class suffer for one child?

I made it a point to visit each room at least twice a day. As I went the rounds I saw the "bad boy" standing in the corner or by the teacher's desk or sitting sullenly by himself where there happened to be room.

"What can I do for you this morning?" I asked as I entered each room.

"I wish you would attend to John. I can't get along with him. He is a constant source of annoyance. He talks and interrupts the lesson. He has talked four times in the last hour. I do not want him in my room anymore."

"John, come with me." John came and I led him to the office.

"What did you do?" I asked.

"I talked to the boy next to me. He asked me a question and I answered."

"How many times did you do this?"

"I don't know. I talked a lot, I guess."

"Why did you disturb the lesson?"

"I don't know."

That is the most persistent answer a "bad boy" gives. No matter what the question or how strong the evidence against him he holds on as long as he can to "I don't know."

"You have got to stop this nonsense," I said finally. "There is only one way to get back to your class. You interrupted the class work. First, you must make good your work. Second, you must make up your mind not to be disorderly again. You're wasting your time and that of your teacher and classmates. Sit down there and think it over. When you have made up your mind let me know."

When John agreed that he had been foolish I went back to the room with him and told the class how sorry I was that they had lost any part of their time and work through John's disorder. I hoped that they would not be troubled again in such a way. John had agreed that he had no right to use his time and theirs in such a silly fashion. He had agreed to make good his work and he would apologize to the class for wasting their time.

A boy, especially a boy who has been master in the street and in the home and would be master in the school, will not risk being humbled before his classmates. Just as long as his offense is an offense against the teacher it is an heroic offense, but when it is an offense against the group, the heroism disappears.

But just to see what might happen next, John refused to "make good." The parent was called in. It was the father, because where John was concerned the mother would not do. . . .

"I can't come here about this boy. This is the second complaint in three weeks. First my wife and now myself. I have lost a day from my work and I can't afford it. What's the matter now? Your teachers are constantly nagging my boy. Why don't you leave him alone? First one teacher and then another. This never happened until you came to this school. I am a taxpayer and I know my rights. I want you to put that boy back in his class, and if you don't, I'll go higher up."

"As a taxpayer you should be the last one to encourage wasting school money."

"I am, I won't stand for it. I'm telling you, I'm going to the commissioner."

"But your son is wasting it. He's been left back twice now. If we cannot get him to get down to work he'll be left back again, which means you've paid three times for something for your boy and haven't received it yet. Besides that, he's wasting other boys' time and they'll be left back and you'll have to pay your share for them and get nothing either. I'm trying to save John's school time and your money, but if you and I together can't make John see it, I am afraid I won't be able to do it alone."

"I can't make him see it? See here, young man, I'm the father of six and I've made them all see it. Send that boy down here."

"No more trouble with John," I said to myself.

Sometimes I found a child under discipline for a trifling offense. I discovered Mary standing in front of the room making believe she liked it.

I asked the teacher what was the trouble.

"Chewing gum," she answered. "I've said they must not bring it into the room and this morning right in the middle of the arithmetic lesson I looked down at Mary and her jaws were going sixty to the minute so I just stood her there. You can sit down now, Mary."

When I got a chance I asked the teacher if she hadn't got the gum chewing a bit out of perspective.

"What do you mean?" she asked.

"Mary lost her arithmetic lesson, didn't she?"

"She surely did and part of her spelling lesson."

"Weren't her lessons very important?—Weren't they what she had come to school for that day?"

"Of course."

"Wouldn't your end have been accomplished if you had signalled to Mary to get rid of the gum and handed her an example to work on the board, putting the emphasis on the duty in hand rather than on her little offense?"

"Maybe you're right," she said, smiling, "I'll think about it that way."

When the disciplinary cases had been systematically looked after some of the pressure was removed from the teacher's life. Less and less frequently did I hear the teacher's voice pitched to the breaking point as she said, "Why don't you behave?"

Gradually the children began to feel that the school was with them and for them and began to assume responsibility for it. They economized school time by arranging and distributing material for the day's work. They began to take care of them-selves in the halls, relieving the teachers of that duty. They ceased marking the walls and picked up the scattered papers without being told to do so.

I saw Peter walk across the yard to pick up a lollipop wrapper and put it in the can and I remembered the day when the yard teacher had ordered Peter to pick up his own luncheon paper and Peter had said, "That's what the janitor's for," and remem-bering I thought, "My school is moving on."

Whenever a problem arose that concerned the school as a whole, I put the problem at the school assembly and whenever a child responded to the school need I spoke of him as one who was serving the school. Gradually this thought of being "square" with one's classmates was carried out of the classroom till it be-came the thought of being "square" with the school.

Henry came to school with his face and body bruised. I asked him what was the matter. He answered some boys had hit him. Upon investigation Henry had been present when the "Flanni-gans" had tried to search some of our smaller children. Henry had protested and then followed up his protest with force and while the smaller children got away Henry "had stayed on the job" as he put it and "been beaten up for his trouble."

"My school is getting on," I thought.

But was it? That day I stopped to talk to a group of teachers who were chatting with my assistant.

"Well, at last I've got discipline." One of the fifth-grade teach-ers was talking. "I've got that class of mine to understand what orders mean. This morning the clerk came in to ask about the transfers of some of the children and said, 'Those living south of the park raise hands!' I counted them. Then I talked to the clerk about William's absence. She was in my room at least seven min-utes. When she left I turned to the class and there were those boys still holding their hands up—you know the way I have them do it, elbow bent and hand close to the shoulder. I said, 'Hands down' just as if I hadn't forgotten them and went ahead. But I certainly was pleased. That's what I call discipline."

Discipline indeed!

Although the emphasis of the discipline was being put largely on the individual as against the group, what each child owed to the class, what each child owed to the school, much of it was still a discipline forced by the conditions of the school. The rod idea was at work. Books, benches, crowded rooms, sitting still, listening; talking only when called upon to recite, teaching where the teacher did the thinking; these conditions have meant and always will mean an imposed discipline, an imposed routine, whereas real discipline is a personal thing, a part of the understanding soul. To replace discipline of teacher-responsibility by the discipline of child-responsibility is a long, slow process.

"My school" had only begun.

III

It was late one afternoon and I walked from room to room through the big silent school building. This was a habit of mine. I was thinking over the events of the day and wondering whether I could ever make the school move, really move. An empty school building and a tired mind! No wonder I felt depressed.

In one of the classrooms I saw a teacher still at work. She was huddled over her desk, her elbows resting on either side of a pile of work, her chin in her hands, weariness and depression in every line of her body.

She looked up at the sound of my step and said in answer to my quizzical smile, "I'm going over the work that has been returned from the office."

"Let's look at it," I said. "It must be very important to keep you like this."

"Oh, no, I must fix it first."

"Fix it? Why, you're through with it, aren't you? The work's been done, examined, and returned and that's the end of it. What more can you do with it? You received some criticism upon it, I suppose?"

"That's just it. That's why I must fix it."

"Let me see it," I persisted.

Reluctantly she pushed the pile of compositions toward me.

On the inner top sheet, in the assistant's neat penmanship, the criticism was inscribed:

1. No. of specimens 48
   Attendance 49
   Why is one missing?
2. 3 blotted papers. Never accept a blotted paper. It shows bad discipline.
3. Many of the e's in this set are closed. Drill on this point.
4. 56 misspelled words. Drill on these.
5. Seven children have too many paragraphs. Only three paragraphs in this grade.
6. Be more particular about margins. One inch in for paragraphs, one-half inch for sentences.
   "Trifles make perfection and perfection is no trifle."
   Do this set over.

I looked up and grinned. A bit relieved, the teacher pushed another pile of papers toward me.

"That's my map. It's Manhattan and I did work hard on it."

Carefully ruled along the sides of each white sheet of drawing paper was a red ink border. Neatly set within this frame was a map of the borough. In the lower right-hand corner was a little compass sign to indicate the directions. All was very, very neat, and very, very dead. On the top sheet in the neat penmanship was written, "This is excellent work. A great improvement over last month's set."

Upon close examination the compositions were all alike. They were written on the same topic. They had the same number of paragraphs. They had the same sentences. It was a story on plants; plants generally, roots, stem, leaves, as close an imitation of a scientific deduction on the abstract life of plants as it was possible for the teacher to make it. Why had they been written at all? There they were, as perfect as could be. Not one of them had the child's language or the child's point of view. Composition is thought and then expression. Here there was no thinking, no child thinking, just a striving for perfect forms. There was neither thought nor language.

I told the teacher to put the papers away, all of them, and go home. She needed the air and the sunshine and what she was doing was of little value to the children.

I determined to look more carefully at this finished work of the classroom.

Some of it I found good. Here and there were signs of life, but most of it was deadly perfect. I remember one set of drawings in particular, a set of cylinders. Each drawing was exactly like the other and what attracted my attention most was the fact that they were placed in exactly the same place on each paper. A faint memory of the dictionary stirred within me and I chuckled to myself.

I sent for the teacher. She was a young teacher in her first year of service. There were about thirty such in the school and upon them I had set my hope for the school's growth.

"These are fine drawings," I said, "very neat and carefully drawn."

She looked pleased.

"I wish you'd tell me now you did them."

"Why, the children did them."

"Of course, I just wanted to know how you managed to get the children to get them all the same size and placed so well on the paper."

"Oh, yes. You know first they made them all ways. Some very long and thin and some short and fat and the sides all crooked. And they were not in the middle of the paper; just a little up or down or sideways, you know?"

"Yes," I agreed. "I know."

"Well, the drawing supervisor told me they must all be the same size and placed correctly on the paper so I thought out a way.

"I took a big needle and pricked little holes in the places

where the four corners of the cylinder were to be and there you are. The rest was easy."

"Anyway," I said to myself as she left me, "she told me."

It was difficult to get teachers away from subject matter, from machinery, and toward children. How could it be otherwise? Had not the teachers been trained to think arithmetic percents, language percents, spelling percents, geography percents? Was not their world a word-world and their thinking a word-thinking?

I tried to improve the teaching by getting away from the accepted treatment of the three R's. These subjects were so thoroughly formalized and logically arranged that no new viewpoint could be carried over through them.

I began by emphasizing subjects that held emotional values: drawing, composition, music, nature, literature. I wanted drawing that expressed the child and not drawing that was made to order. I wanted ideas expressed in color, movement, fun and not lines, ideas and not perfect papers, every one alike. I wanted composition that expressed the child and was not made to order; two sentences for the third grade, two paragraphs for the fourth grade, simple sentences in the fifth grade, complex sentences in the sixth grade, and so on indefinitely. I wanted nature that would make the child's heart warm with sympathy, that would make the child dig and plant and be glad of the earth smells, that would make him talk to the dumb beasts and yearn to care for them, that would make him laugh to feel the snow and the rain and the wind beating on his face.

The feeling for the things that I wanted was rather more definite than the knowledge of how to attain the desired results. I planned, however, as best I knew how. I watched my opportunities. I went into the classrooms and helped the teachers with their work and the teachers, it seemed to me, responded. They smiled. They were interested. They showed confidence in the newer point of view.

"We are getting on," I thought.

Then something happened. One of the assistants came to me and said, "I want to talk to you." Her tone signified the unusual and I listened intently.

"I must leave this school. You and I do not agree. You are putting the whole weight of the school on the nonessentials. The teachers are putting all their energy on music, nature, composition, and drawing. I can't get the arithmetic up to the standard in the time that's left."

"Aren't the teachers giving the allotted time to the arithmetic?"

"Yes, but they give just that and no more. I mean that they do not bring the pressure to bear on it that they did and the work is falling off. It's according to your direction, and as you and I cannot agree on that point I am going to another school."

"I'm not getting on," said another teacher. "I don't know what to do. The superintendent is coming and I'm afraid we won't be ready, especially in Nature Study. You tell us to work for the children and forget ourselves but we can't forget the superintendent. I can't get the facts he wants without drill and I can't drill and teach the way you say."

"But I believe you can teach, really teach the child to think and enjoy the work, and at the same time give the examiner the kind of work he wants," I said.

"Will you come and hear my nature lesson on the Robin?"

"Gladly," I said.

"I give it first thing in the morning," she told me.

I was on hand promptly. There was no sign of anything in the room that looked like a robin unless it was the plump little lad in the first seat who kept looking up eagerly, open mouthed, into the teacher's face, ready to catch each word.

"Now, children, we are going to talk about a bird. One you all like to hear about. He's a cheerful little fellow with a brown coat and a red breast, and two bright eyes, and he sings, cheerily, cheerily! What's his name?"

Silence.

"I'm afraid you're not thinking hard, children. Think hard.

What's his name? He has a brown coat, a red vest, two bright eyes, and he sings cheerily, cheerily—What do you call him?"

Then the boy in the first seat spoke up.

"Tony," he said.

Tony was an Italian sweeper, who unfortunately for the smooth progress of the lesson answered the description to a nicety.

The teacher turned to me, her face flushed and her eyes shining. "There, you see—I tried to make the lesson interesting and that's what happens. I can't do it your way."

"But maybe that isn't my way."

"Why, that's what you told me to do. I'm sure I don't know what you mean."

"If you'll come to me during the day, I'll try to tell you."

When she came, I said, "There are robins in the park just across the street?"

"Yes, lots of them."

"Suppose you meet the class under the big oak tree in the morning and look for robins. Watch them until you and the children know as much about them as one can learn by looking—size, color, bill, food, the funny little tripping walk, the cock of the eye, and the turn of the head; the nest and the babies you'll have to get from pictures, but having real birds in your mind, that will come easy. Then talk over what you've seen and learned. Let everybody say his say sometime or other. Tell them a story, have them sing a song about Robin Red Breast.

"Then when you have all the facts about him select those that are most worthwhile, and present them as the robin story. You'll find you'll need very little drill."

Doubtfully she shook her head.

As she started to walk out of the room I could see the shadow of the coming examination still in her countenance.

"And by the way—you know it's Tony that wears the vest—not Robin Redbreast. Don't worry. Outline the lesson again and then come back and let me go over it with you."

IV

The average parent thinks of education largely in terms of books. The poorer the people are the more apt they are to overvalue the traditional work of the school. The school is the place to learn from books and the child must not waste time doing anything else. Time spent in play is waste. Time spent on music, cooking, stories, dramatics, dancing, wood, clay, is waste. These are the fads and frills and while desirable are altogether unnecessary. What the child needs is to get on in the world, to get a job that gets him away from hard work. To do that the child must know how to read, to write, to spell, to count. He need not know anything about music, hammers, needles, food.

Parents have been trained, as have the teachers, to think of school as a place where the children are made to obey, to memorize, made to repeat lessons.

I felt that we had to win the parents as well as the teachers if the changes we were making, our emphasis on the "fads and frills" of education, were to be accepted in the homes.

I should have known that the people believed in the sufficiency of the three R's. They had not realized that the children of the city were losing all chance of firsthand experience with life. They had not realized that the schools must hasten to furnish the opportunity for them on the playground and in the shops. Only when there was a better public conception of what the schools should do would school life really change.

When I cut down home study so as to give the child some relief from the pressure of the curriculum and thus allow them more time to grow, Sam's mother came to me, wrath in her eyes.

"Good morning. I've just run in for a minute this morning to ask how it is that Sam has no homework to speak of. Just a few examples and five words and a little reading. Sometimes he has a couple of sentences. He does them in no time. Now in the last school he was in he used to have work enough to keep him a couple of hours. He'd come in from school, do his errands, wash up for supper. After supper he'd work until it was time to go to bed."

But I protested, "We think Sam is doing very well. There is no need for his working two hours at home. If he works to his full capacity for five hours a day, that is enough for a little fellow ten years old. Don't you think so?"

"Well, I don't know. He doesn't have enough to do to keep him quiet. He bothers the family and we don't like it at all. Last night he bothered me until I had to get up and get him stuff to make an air thing. I don't know what it is—something he wants to make fly. Now he'd be better off doing some long-division examples, and I think the teacher ought to have more to do than tell him stories about flying machines, anyway. He can learn that when he's older if he wants to."

"I'm sorry you feel that way about it. The child has all the book study he needs, I think, and if anything, too much homework. I think Sam needs sunshine and clean sports and a chance in the open. He is going to fly kites to get ready for the kite-flying contest to be held in the park next month."

"Then I want you to give me a transfer," she answered with decision. "My boy needs an education. He can't afford to waste time like a rich man's son. I'll put him in another school where he can learn something."

And nothing I could say would change her belief. Aerial navigation was too far from the three R's for Sam. He must stay nearer the earth.

Even the babies in the first grade, the infant class, did not escape.

"Don't you find Aaron ahead of his class?" an aggressive mother asked me.

"I find him a very bright little boy."

"Yes, I knew you would. I taught him myself. He can read the whole of 'The Red Hen' and count to one hundred without a mistake. When are you going to promote him?"

I temporized. "I rather think Aaron can go ahead with his class

next January." (It was September.) "Yes, if he grows as he promises to, he will be ready for promotion with his class."

"But he can read the whole of 'The Red—'"

"Yes, I know, but, you see, the school stands for more than just
the few intellectual facts that the curriculum imposes upon your
child. He needs time to live, to grow, to be a child with other
children. He needs time to sense the curriculum as well as memorize it. That can only be done by living it with his teacher and
his classmates. If to teach the few facts of the curriculum were all
we were here for, the school would better be closed."

By this time the mother began to feel maybe she hadn't it
right, after all, and went away shaking her head and sighing.

"School was different in my time. We *learned*. We got 'what
for' if we didn't."

"This is the principal?" puffed a little ball of a man as he rolled
into the office. "I came to see about my boy's, Fred's teacher.
Maybe you think she is a good teacher. I don't know it. She keeps
my boy in. She tells him stories. Fred comes home. He walks
round and round the rooms and says words like the actors. Tell
her to please stop—I don't like it. I don't like it."

"Does Fred like it?" I asked.

"He likes?" and there was fire in his eyes. "Yes, he likes it like
anything. That he likes and nothing else. Why, if she wants to
teach Fred extra, don't she give him more arithmetic? That is
good for Fred when he grows up. He goes then to business and
he knows nothing. Whose fault? Fred is not good in his lessons.
My brother's son is two classes ahead and he is the same age.
Fred should study hard. He should not waste his brain on humbug. Tell her to please stop. Fred needs his senses for reading
and writing."

"Would you like to see the teacher? She might explain," I
suggested.

"Yes, I will see her. She must not tell stories. She must not
waste time. Fred will be big soon, very soon."

The teacher came.

"You Fred's teacher?" he said as soon as he saw her. "Well, you must not tell stories, I don't like it. I want an education for my boy, not foolishness. Stories are humbug."

"But we have these stories after school hours when all the required work is done," pleaded the teacher.

"Yes, yes, but give him some more examples if you want to help him along—but please, my dear young lady, don't tell stories. I don't like it."

Then the grandmother of Katherine came in, a hearty, cheery, plump-cheeked, steel-bowed spectacled grandmother, who seated herself with firmness and began without preface:

"Why doesn't your teacher teach the children to spell?"

Her eyes were challenging—the clear, clipped tones hinted, "No nonsense now, I'm here to be shown."

"What class is Katherine in?"

"First grade, room 7."

"Oh, we do not teach spelling in 1A."

"And well I know you don't. I'm glad you're truthful. Why don't you? Here Katherine can read the whole of 'The Red Hen' and not a word can the poor child spell, much less know a letter. Every night I'm trying to pound it into her, and we're as far from it now as when we began. What's wrong, anyway?"

"You see," I tried to explain, "we don't teach reading just that way. Suppose you spend an hour in the classroom and see how we do it?"

"Surely, surely, I want you to show me."

At the end of the period, grandmother came back.

"Well, that's a fine young woman—and healthy, I'll say that for her. And the children do read well. But *I* learned to spell when I was six, and it never hurt me."

"Or helped you," I thought, but silence was better than speech this time, and grandmother went home silenced but not convinced.

The next complaint came from an entirely different source. This time it was Mary Ann's mother who spoke. Mary Ann was in the

"defectives' class" and would stay in that class outside and inside
school until the earth closed over her.

Mary Ann's mother was a picturesque figure in her sport skirt,
an antiquated basque with a brave row of steel buttons down the
front, a pert sailor hat sailing under an aggressive quill. In her
earnestness she went directly to the teacher.

"Teacher dear, Mary Ann's doing foine, foine. She hasn't tore
the baby since I don't know whin, and she's getting that civil you
wouldn't believe it. Hardly a bad word out of her mouth now,
and she goes to Sunday School with Bettie. I'm proud and thankful to ye. But that's not what I came to ask ye. Just drop them
bastits you're having her makin', and them drills she fiddles her
time away in and teach her to read. Teach her to read so she can
learn her catechism and save her immortal soul and then I don't
care. But in God's name, teach her to read."

And Mary Ann's mother broke down and wept.

There you are. From the highest to lowest, the book and the
book knowledge shall save you. It shall even save your soul.

Many parents believe that this is education. They covet knowledge, book knowledge for their children. Rich and poor alike want
their children done up in little packages, ready to show, ready to
boast of. They fear freedom, they fear to let the child grow by
himself. Because the parents want this sort of thing, the school is
built to suit—a book school—one room like another, one seat
like another, each child like his neighbor.

3

Outside the School

I

At the end of the first term the school was promoted. A mass of children went from our sixth-year grade to the seventh grade of a neighboring school. A new group from the fifth grade of our neighbor's school was promoted to our sixth grade.

At the end of the second term the school was promoted again. We lost the older children upon whom the responsibility for school spirit depended and we got the younger children in exchange. The two groups crossed and recrossed on their way to and from the two schools.

What could we do with a shifting school population?

A mother came into the school one morning. She wanted "to see the principal." I was then on my rounds of the building. She waited because she wanted "to see the principal on very important business." When I came she began. It was the concrete presentation of the protest that the teachers and I had been feeling.

"I'm sick of the name of school. Just see this for yourself. Is it reasonable? Is it just? And to think that I should live to say such a thing with two of my boys graduates of public school and one now in high school. But I must say it, I've stood it long enough. Something has got to be done or I shall go crazy.

"It's this way. I ask you to do something for me. Thomas goes to the Jefferson Avenue School. He is in 8A. Mary goes to the First Avenue School and John, the smallest, comes here.

"When they come home there is a fight. Each one cheers for his own. Last night Mary came home with her school colors and Thomas said they were no good. Then there was talking and crying and Mary lost her temper and she had to be put to bed. The father blames me. It's the same with all the mothers on the block. With the children here and there we don't know what to do."

Here she stopped and felt nervously about for her handkerchief.

I recalled the visits of the other parents who had come objecting to this same condition.

"Now I want them to go all together," she resumed. "One school is as good as another, but three is too many. The big child could keep an eye on the little one and help her across the car tracks. The little one is a bit slow in lessons and if the big boy tries to help him he says, 'We don't do it that way in our school,' and then there is more fighting. If they went to the same school they could help each other.

"Now I want you to stop this foolishness and put them all in the same school. What kind of a family will this be, I'm asking you? And that's not all. They go at different times—I'm getting meals all day long. No use going to see teachers. It's a day's trip. Please transfer them to one school."

Here the mother collapsed. This was the longest speech she had ever made.

She was right. The time had come to put a stop to this "foolishness."

"Please transfer these children to the same school," or "Keep them there!" was a good slogan. If that could be done we would save the changes of both children and teachers.

Surely there must be some mistake. It was never intended that the smallest children should be shifted about in this way. It was never intended that this school should be the helpless thing that it was.

I said to those whom I could get to listen, "Unity and continuity are the two potent elements in the life of the school. The tendency to break up the school is not wholesome. I believe the

full-graded school where the school life of the child is continuous is the best school for children. I believe the children stay longer
in such a school and do the work faster and more thoroughly.

"Do you know," I went on, "that this school has at present six
different distinct, district lines? Is there any good reason why
this school should not retain its children through all its grades
and prevent the waste that comes through needless transfers?"

The kindly old janitor of the school advised me when he saw
what I was about.

"Don't stir them up," he said; "don't stir them up. I have been
in this business for thirty years and I have found stirring them up
won't do. If they say it is raining, put up your umbrella, but don't
stir them up."

I did not think the janitor was right. When I failed to get my
point over I said, "They do not understand."

When parents came to me with complaints, I sent them on to
the school authorities. "The people will explain and the explanation will help," I thought. But the authorities resented being
stirred up and they did nothing.

A member of the local board came to see me.

"What's the matter with you anyway?" he said rather sharply.
"You're not playing the game. You knew this was a six-year school
when you came to it. Then as soon as you get here you begin stirring up trouble. You're only a beginner, you'll get your full school
when your turn comes. If you can't wait, get a transfer."

"You don't understand," I said, taken aback. "It's for the children I'm asking this, not for myself. This organization is bad for
them. Adjust it and I'll take any school you like."

"That's all in your eye. I know better," he said.

The protest was useless. I felt that school people were not going to help me, either by convincing me that I was wrong or by
active assistance when I was right. Was I facing the same conditions as a principal that I had faced as a teacher? "Do what you
are told to do. Do what the rest are doing."

Strangest of all was the fact that they were thoroughly honest in their position. It was the point of view. They saw a school for administration. I saw a school for the "all-around" development of children.

I wanted opportunity for the masses, the best schools for the crowds, the best teachers for the heaviest load. I thought in terms of service, they in terms of tradition.

The changes that had been made in the school organization had been made to benefit the older children. The best teachers, the best buildings, the smallest classes, the finest equipment were provided for the few at the top. There was no top to my school, and there were no facilities of equipment, no shops, no gymnasium, no playground—only classrooms. It did not matter whether our children stayed in our school or were transferred out of it. It did not matter much what happened to the youngest children. The tradition in school management was and still is that the older children are the ones most worthwhile; that the teachers of these older children are the superior teachers; that the principal of a full-graded school has a higher standing than one of a six-year school; that the president of a college is superior to the principal of a high school.

Soon the teachers who sought promotion went into the high school or the full-graded school, because these schools offered higher salaries and larger opportunities for professional growth.

What chance then had this school of becoming a real school? What chance had this school for continuity of life? What influence could its training show upon the conduct of children?

What was I to do?

II

The daily disciplinary records had begun to show up the few steady offenders. The same names appeared with almost the same complaint.

The worst among them was the leader with his gang. I found they had headquarters in a forsaken mansion. They had stripped it of any saleable fixtures and used the money for cigarettes, candy, soda, carfare, and shows.

Sometimes they had a fight with some of the other boys in the neighborhood. The pitched battles took place in the vacant lots and frequently in the park. Then there would be a rush of protesting parents to the school and the station house. The police would charge down upon the contending armies and they would disappear across the lots into cellars and over roofs.

What was school to them, when, armed with stones and carrying shields made of pot covers or old wash boilers pounded flat, they sallied forth to attack a neighboring gang!

The leader had caught my notice by having had numerous charges of fighting made against him. He had carried his street battles into the school and the teacher and the class had to suffer the consequent annoyance and inconvenience.

The freight yard with its busy traffic had the greatest attraction for him. Something was going on there all the time. The cars clanging, grinding, bumping! The brakemen running along the top of the cars, shouting and waving their arms! The trucks, the horses, the thrill of an accident, and the crowd that gathered about the swift-rushing ambulance—here was life. Expeditions, thefts, stolen rides, broken limbs, what chances for adventure!

One night there was nothing to do—no fruit stand to turn over, no peddler to bait, so he led his friends to the freight yard. A mass of bulging bags containing malt was discovered. These were cut and some of the malt carried away to a cellar "den."

The police traced the miscreants to a fifth-year class. The officer who came took the ringleader and started off. Before they had gone ten feet there was a flash of grey, and the boy flew down the hall, scarcely making a sound, and a hurtling mass of blue pounded after him. The prisoner was gone.

A tearful youngster appealed to me, "Will you please make the Flannigans let us alone?" he wailed.

"Who are the Flannigans?" I asked.

"They are a gang of Irishers that fight us. Every day they fight us. Last night they lassoed my brother and took him to their den and my father and the police had to get him out. My father says you should get the leader. His name is Flannigan. That ain't his real name, either. It's Arente. He is in 2 A."

"In grade 2 A and you are in 6 B?"

"Yes, sir. He is big and his gang is bigger. They even work. We haven't any show with them."

"I'll have to see about them," I comforted him. "It's too bad."

During the day this lad's mother came in to see me. "I thought you were going to see about the Flannigans? Issie told you about them this morning," she said.

"Yes," I returned, "but I've been very busy today and haven't had a chance to see Arente yet."

"Then that's why. On the way out at noon he licked Issie for telling you and says he'll do him something if he tells anymore."

I sent for Arente, who promptly dissolved into tears. That didn't help any. Tears came easily to him. I sent him home for his mother and asked Issie's mother to wait. In a short time mother and son appeared, and I told the story.

"Well," she said aggressively, "this happened on the street, didn't it? What have you got to do with it? I guess if you attend to your job inside school it will give you enough to do."

"But," interrupted the other mother, "he licked my Issie."

"Sure he did," responded the plumed lady, "and serve himself well right. Let Issie fight his own battles. I don't come here about what happens to my son. If he gets a black eye that's his bad luck. What happens on the street is none of the school's business. You needn't send for me to settle your son's scraps," and she swept grandly out.

"No wonder he licks Issie," gasped the remaining visitor. "She's fierce. Try and do your best for my boy that he isn't killed."

I agreed to try and showed Issie's mother out. Then I sat down to think it over. I consulted Arente's teacher about the street fights. She laughed heartily at me—"What, a sixth-year boy complaining about a second-year boy! He doesn't belong in a public school with the boys. He needs a nurse and a perambulator."

"But for some reason or other," I interposed, "Arente is backed up by some older boys, really young men, and it isn't exactly a fair fight, you see."

"It happened on the street, didn't it?" she inquired in a puzzled tone. "What have we to do with it? We can't control the street life of these children. We couldn't if we wished to, and it's really none of our business.

"I'll speak to Arente but it won't do much good. If Arente doesn't beat Issie somebody else will. On the street, it's lick or be licked. How's the school going to help it?"

"How indeed?" I wondered. "It's not the school's business. We stop at the street door. It's not the home's business. That stops at the door. The street is the third powerful factor in education and we know nothing about it."

Turning over the leaves of my Happenings Book I selected the following:

"Complaint of candy peddler. Boys pulled his beard and took some candy."

"Mrs. Wellon reported that a little girl went into her house by fire-escape window and took eleven cents out of a teacup."

"Janitor of apartment house says boys tipped ash can down cellar stairs."

"Sign painter—very angry—charged boys with taking away ladder and leaving him perched thirty feet above sidewalk."

"A letter from a lady suggesting that I stand at the front door of my school to receive the children as they enter and praise those who have clean faces, well-brushed hair and boots. She has noticed children entering our school who were not well groomed. There are thirteen entrances to this school and four thousand children."

"Edison company requests us to cooperate in the protection of their light globes."

"The delicatessen man says Rachel steals a dill pickle every day."

"Received an official circular asking our help in the protection of public property, street, lights, parks, public buildings, books, etc.

"Mrs. Wenc wants Fritz to come in the front door so Michael can't punch him."

"So," I said to myself, 'My school' is different? Well, it isn't. It's the same old school. The teachers and children—the streets and the troubles—have different names but they're the same all over the world. Home shuts the door and by that simple action closes out the world. School shuts the door and concerns itself no further. But the street roars on, its life at full tide, sweeping the children by our closed doors."

Ethical principles! The old questions clung to me with all the tenacity of a first impression, "Is the teacher responsible for what the child does out of school? If this is not the teacher's province how can the teacher ever know that her work counts in the life of the child?"

III

I had met a few, a very few parents who had come into the school on rare occasions. They had come for the most part objecting to something the school was doing. But what of the great mass, who were they?

They were parents who were ignorant, almost, of the school's existence. Some of them did not know the teacher's name, nor the child's class, nor the number of the school. They hardly knew where the school was. Perhaps they had sent a neighbor to register the child in the "baby" class and had never been near the school. What did they know of the school? What did they care?

What did we know of their homes? What did we care?

We would know, we would care, I determined. We would go to them and learn what was beyond their closed doors.

There was Hyman. He was dirty, more than dirty. Word was

sent home that Hyman should have a bath. No bath was given. Dirt reaches a climax. It did in this case.

Then the teacher said, "Hyman, if no one else will wash you, I will. But washed you must be."

Hyman led the way cheerfully. There was a short journey through crowded streets, a dark hallway, long flights of stairs, then Hyman's home. The living room was kitchen and dining room as well. Hyman's mother was at the tubs. On the table in one corner was a cut-up chicken, the night's dinner; close to the chicken was a pair of newly mended shoes. There was a loaf of bread with the heart pulled out of it and a dish of butter showing finger marks. Odd dishes, a coffeepot with streaks of coffee down its sides, and some freshly washed clothes filled the rest of the table. Children's clothes were all about.

There were five schoolchildren in this family. Each on his way from school dropped his belongings, helped himself to a chunk of bread and a dab of butter, and made for the street, the only available place to pursue his right to "life, liberty, and the pursuit of happiness."

"Yes, I know, teacher," said the mother limply, "I know Hyman is dirty. He won't wash for me. Maybe he will for you."

Through the kitchen into the bathroom went Hyman and his teacher. The bathroom was the family storeroom. Everything was there that anybody discarded—a couple of hats, an empty box or two, shoes, old clothes. These were piled on the floor, the tub cleaned, and Hyman with the teacher's help got into the bath, the first in many days.

Then the teacher went home, thinking, "What's the good of school, just school, to Hyman? He needs to grow. He needs to learn to be clean more than he needs to learn to spell. Congestion, tenements, dirt, neglect! What chance has Hyman to be a fine American citizen?"

"I want to tell you about a home I visited yesterday," a teacher said. "Percy hasn't done any real work since he entered my class so I thought I'd call on his mother. She made an appointment for me and I went. She was dressed as though for a party and when I apologized for detaining her she said, 'Oh, not at all. It's my bridge club day but it's early yet. What about Percy? Bothering you? Children are a bother, aren't they? How do you ever get on with forty or fifty of them? One kills me.'

"'Percy isn't doing any school work,' I said bluntly. 'He acts as if he needed sleep, too. He never does his homework.'

"'Oh, Mercy! What's homework? Lessons? Of course he doesn't do any at home. Isn't school enough?'

"'It is for some boys who work. But Percy works neither at home nor at school.'

"'M'm. It's too bad. You see we entertain a lot. We are fond of having our friends about us; good for children to meet people, don't you think? Gives them an air.'

"'But does the child sleep?'

"'Oh, of course, you silly child, he sleeps. Let me give you a cup of tea. No? Maybe you'd have a cocktail? What can one of-fer a schoolmarm? So glad to have seen you. Thanks so much for your interest in Percy! He comes from a good family. He'll come out all right. Don't worry. So glad. Good-bye.'"

Then there was Ruth. The teachers found her intractable at times because of an overwhelming desire to take control of the classroom. On the whole she was worthwhile and intelligent. What was the trouble with Ruth?

Ruth was ten and very, very wise. She had glorious red hair, braided and bound like a coronet. She looked at you out of beau-tiful, green eyes and talked in slow, monotonous tones, the result of much experience with the direct facts of life. Once Ruth had taken off her little red flannel petticoat and waved it in the faces of the Cossacks who had come to search the house for rev-olutionary literature. This little demonstration had hurried the family's departure from Russia. Somehow she had grasped the idea of going straight to headquarters when she wanted anything.

"I hope you won't mind, but I want to ask your advice," she an-nounced one day. "It isn't about school."

Ruth really never wanted advice. She always felt competent to give it so I waited in silence.

"Well, you see, it's this way. There are eight of us at home and father, he sits home and won't go to work only when he likes it and then he gives my mother only two dollars a week. That isn't much for a room and meals, especially now. Well, I wouldn't mind his not paying more money, if he would only leave my mother and the children alone. No, he sits there and complains and swears to my brothers and sisters. Such languages isn't good for children to hear. He is getting worse and worse every day, and my mother cries and I can't bear to see my mother cry. You don't know how hard my mother works.

"There is Abe. He is eight, but he is a little stupid and very weak and can't eat regular food. And my big sister that goes to work in the fur shop downtown and gets home all tired out. You could hardly believe how hard she works.

"And my father makes all this trouble. He plays cards at night with his friends that came from the other side with him, the same country he came from. When the men come to play cards, we must stay up late, and that's not good for us. I can't stand it any longer."

Here Ruth stopped talking and looked at me expectantly.

Still I waited, merely lifting an inquiring eyebrow.

"I took advice," she resumed, "and went before the judge and told him everything. Now had I the right? The judge asked me if we wanted to put him out. I said no, he was my father, but I wanted the judge to make him stop using bad languages. The judge did, and told me to come to him in case there was any more trouble."

"How has your father been since?" I asked her when I had sufficiently recovered.

"Very well. He does not talk much, but he looks as if he wanted to. I don't care; I know what's good for him."

"Is he to give you any more money?"

"Yes, the judge said he must give half his salary at least and he must work, and be good, and be proud of his children."

❖   ❖   ❖

I found a boy in a classroom after school hours. His shirt was full of flowers that other children had brought to the teacher.

"What are you going to do with them?"

"Take them home and hide them."

Why hide them? His mother would not let him take the flowers home. She did not want him to steal flowers.

I went to see his father. He knew his boy took flowers not only from the teacher but also from the florist and from the park. He would punish the boy as he had done many times before. I could see for myself by examining the boy's body. He would whip him more now than ever.

"What can I do?" he went on. "I go out to work all day. I have three children that go to school. I make a dollar and a half a day when it does not rain; I have to pay fourteen dollars a month rent. I want my boy to learn. I give him plenty to eat though beans are ten cents a pound. I try to make him study and he goes out stealing flowers and disgraces me."

"A dollar and fifty cents a day, when it does not rain." I saw the man's torn shoes, his shabby clothes and knotted fingers. I saw the boy's skinny body and his starving soul craving for the sweet earth flowers. Was it the child's fault?

"Please help me. Do something for me," pleaded a sixteen-year-old girl just out of school. "My little brother makes such a fuss at home! When he does not like his food, he pulls the tablecloth on the floor and breaks the dishes. When a young man comes to see me, my brother makes such trouble that he never comes back. Now I am getting along in years. I'll be seventeen next birthday. I am losing my chances. He threw the sofa pillows out of the window. I must take from my savings to buy more pillows and dishes. How can I save up for a husband?"

"Please make my boy clean himself before he comes to school. He won't do it for me."

"Please talk to Herbert about hitting his little brother. You have such influence over him."

"Put my boy away. He is no good. He steals my money."

"Solomon is at home stamping his feet. He will not go for me. Please send the officer."

"Please tell Dorothy she must take her medicine. She will do it for you. It's a bother to you I know, but I'll make it all right with you."

Inadequate, isolated homes, forever closing their doors and forever begging us to come in!

IV

On one side of the school was the road, dusty, badly kept, and constantly used. Across the street was the park, beautiful and fresh at first but as the population increased, abused and neglected more and more.

On the other side ran the elevated trains that disturbed us all. Assembly exercises in the morning had to stop to let the trains go by. Classroom recitations had to stop, too, for there was no competition. The children and the teachers got the habit of waiting in the middle of a sentence as the roar began, swelled—ceased.

The school district reached across the park to the east where lived many families who owned their own houses. These were the first residents, the lovers of grass and open spaces, of home and family traditions. It extended westward four blocks to the tracks of the railroad and north and south almost a quarter of a mile each way. A wide area this. Scattered about were empty lots, fences—long stretches of fences, empty houses and flats. The neighborhood was in a state of transition from a dignified provincial suburb to a mass of tenements. There was a group of people who came from the southern part of the city each spring that their children might enjoy the open spaces of the neighborhood. They remained until fall when they returned to their steam-heated flats. This made an unstable community in the school and in the neighborhood. Each time they came fewer of them returned and the tenements grew in number.

This meant that most of our children came from little two-, three-, and four-room flats, strung along block upon block. In such homes there was little time or room for play, work, or fun. As the crowds came the tenements increased and poured their tenants out upon the sidewalks and streets. The street corner, the curb, the candy shop, the pool room, the dance hall were becoming the social centers of the district.

There was a mixture of races. These were people who had come from various countries of Europe and they differed in their attitude toward ethics, society, religion, education, cleanliness. These differences isolated the various groups, the families, and the blocks.

These parents did not understand the newer conditions of life. They did not understand the city. They did not understand the school. They did not understand the older residents.

In their turn they, too, were misunderstood, even by their own children. The child saw in the rush of the school life the idea of getting on. In school he saw life in a white collar, fine clothes, and an easy job. Home was not like this.

Michael was one of the brightest and most promising among the boys. He was a yard monitor. He came to school early and stayed late. He helped the teachers attend to supplies and hang pictures. Whatever the work in hand, Michael was first assistant.

A neighbor brought Michael's mother in to see me. She turned to her friend and spoke in a foreign tongue and the neighbor answered, and turned to me, saying, "She speaks no English. I have come to talk to you for her."

"That's too bad. I thought Michael was born in this city?" I said.

"Oh, yes, they've been in this country fifteen years, but she never learned the language. She's religious and doesn't go around much."

Michael's mother was anxiously watching our faces while we talked and now she spoke again to the neighbor.

"She says to tell you that she wants to see Michael."

Michael was sent for and came into the office with his usual cheerful willingness. When he saw his mother he stopped. She went toward him. Michael backed against the wall, his face sullen and embarrassed. His mother talked pleadingly. She put

her hand on his shoulder and he pushed it off rudely. Then his
mother sank into a chair and began to cry softly.

Michael stood against the wall scowling down at his shoes. I
looked on, wondering what it could be about. The neighbor began to talk.

"It's a pity. It's a shame. Mickee, you shouldn't treat your
mother that way."

"She shouldn't come here," muttered Michael.

The neighbor looked from Michael to the weeping woman
and anger shone in her face as she turned to me.

"You think Michael is a good boy, don't you? You like him.
Well, I don't. You think you do a lot for him by keeping him in
school all day long and letting him run all over for the teachers.
You're just spoiling him. You're only making him selfish. He
thinks he's too good to talk to his own mother. That's what you're
doing if you want to know the truth."

Then turning to Michael she said, "If you belonged to me you
wouldn't act like that. I'd fix you."

Michael lifted his head ready to answer, but, catching my eye,
resumed his sullen attitude again.

"You can go to your room now, Michael. Come in to see me after hours," I said to his great relief.

"I'd wish," the neighbor broke in, "you would take a stick to
that kid's back. His mother can do nothing more with him. I'm
sorry for her. She came from Russia years ago. She was quiet and
stayed in the house. Michael is ashamed of her because she can't
talk English. He makes fun of her clothes. When there is a
school party he doesn't even tell her. Her husband learned English and all the American ways quickly. So did the children. Now
her husband is ashamed of her and he lives by himself. Michael
goes to see him and lots of times he stays two or three days. His
mother hasn't seen him this week. That's why she came here, to
beg him to come home to her."

Here were children and parents living their lives apart. These
children were ashamed because their parents did not speak or
look like Americans. How could I help the children in my school

respond to the dreams of their fathers? How could I get the fathers to share in the work of building a school for their children?

The parents often misunderstood the motives of the school in dealing with their children. Especially was this true of the parents whose children were fitted for manual rather than for intellectual labor.

When their fourteen-year-old boys and girls who had almost reached their full physical growth and had difficulty in making the fifth grade were placed in a special class in which the emphasis was put on the fundamentals of learning because they would soon have to go out and work for a living, the parents came to protest.

I did not blame them for protesting, although my reason was different from theirs. Already these children had had too much of the fundamentals. Their mentalities had foundered on the sacred three R's. In these average special classes, instead of less of the three R's, the children got more of them. It was like taking a drowning man out of a lake and throwing him into the sea.

But the parents protested not because these children were being given more reading, writing, and arithmetic, but because the special class meant that the child who was put there was an outcast from the normal school life. He would soon have to go to work because he had no brains for books.

In the country they came from this question would not have arisen. The children would have gone to the farm or the factory as their fathers for generations had gone. But it was to avoid that future they had come to this new land, and when we were obliged to say to some of them that their children would never be able to become doctors or lawyers or priests but they would and should become workingmen and -women, they were bitter in their denunciation of the school.

So it was in matters of health. Parents who had been brought up in the country, where there was no noise, no confusion, no confinement, where the food came directly from the soil, were somewhat at a loss to appreciate why it was that their children so often were ill.

They could not understand that the noise of the city life and the speed of city work, the effect of canned foodstuff and adulterated food products, were factors in the lives of their children. They could not, therefore, understand why their children could not grow as they had.

Having been in the habit of trusting nature, they declared when the school required medical attention, "The child will grow out of it. I never had such diseases and why should my child?" Even when they seemed convinced that medical attention was necessary, they still had little faith in what was told them, or in the doctor and his medicine.

The school alone could do nothing. It was not organized with the idea of a maximum spiritual and intellectual growth.

The home alone could do nothing. It was isolated, antagonistic, indifferent. It shut its eyes fearing, distrusting, hoping for better things but doing nothing. The more it lived by itself the less able it became to hold the children close to itself.

I had learned that education was a matter of cooperation between parents and teachers. Conduct, self-expression, meant action in the street and home. Moral education meant group reaction.

The problems of my school, therefore, loomed up as the problems of our community. The transfers of our teachers and of our children, the equipment of the building, the curriculum, were not only school problems but also community problems. Unless the people knew about and shared in the education of their children the schools would be inefficient. To save the school and the home from becoming cloistered, self-centered, the culture of children would have to be a cooperative effort between the parents and the teachers.

4

The Parents at Work

I

"How did you begin?"

I don't know exactly how I began. I began as so many others did without realizing that I was beginning anything unusual. I began slowly, hesitatingly, making many mistakes as I went.

"How did you begin?"

Does not that very question try to force a tabulated, logically arranged answer that may be applied like a formula to any situation? Is it not more important to know why the school began, and how the work grew, and the value of what the school learned while it was growing?

I explained to the teachers that we needed the parents. How we were going to get them was another matter. I have a feeling that we started by noting the men and women who seemed to take some interest in the school life of their children. I distinctly remember that we studied the various neighborhood groups to discover who the leaders were, that we singled out those who objected most to what the children were doing in their street time. Slowly, almost unconsciously, the neighborhood people came in touch with the school and with each other.

Our primary task was to hear the people talk. The more they talked, the sooner we were able to see what they were like and what they had to give to the school. We were good listeners and when we saw that a neighbor's vital interests touched some phase of common social growth, we knew that neighbor had something to give that the school needed.

Early one morning, before opening exercises, a gentleman came in and said he must see me at once. He was greatly excited and paced up and down the office as he talked.

"Two of my boys come to this school so I think you ought to be interested in what concerns their welfare and whatever goes on in the neighborhood concerns them mightily."

Here was a man with a point of view. I listened intently.

"Yesterday one of them might have been killed by one of your pupils. The milkman leaves his cases of empty bottles in the vacant lot opposite my house. Yesterday afternoon a gang of boys fought the children on the block with those bottles. They threw them at each other's heads, sir. I tell you it's outrageous. My boys were coming home peaceably when some of those ruffians attacked them with empty bottles—glass bottles. It's murderous, I tell you. Fun's fun but this is no fun." And he brought his clenched fist down smartly on his outstretched palm. "What's the school doing? Can you offer us parents no better protection for our children than this?"

Drawing himself to his full height and speaking more earnestly, if possible, he rallied me to a sense of my duty. "The public school is or ought to be the greatest force for good in the community. If it's going to stand by and see these children of foreigners actually murder our children—the children of generations of Americans who gave their lives for their flag and their country—then this nation is lost, sir. As a parent and a citizen I call upon you to do your duty. Search out the miscreants and mete out fit punishment for them. Skinning's too good for them."

Advancing to the desk shelf that separated us, he punctuated his rapid phrases with sharp taps of his fingers. "When I went to school they used to teach the children respect for law and order and above all a regard for truth. But the schools these days have no time to teach law and order. They have no time to teach the simple adherence to the truth."

"But," I suggested, before he could begin again, "perhaps some of this misbehavior, which as you state occurs outside the school, is due to the lack of care and influence of the home folk?"

"Maybe, maybe, a little of it. But work isn't done by shifting the responsibility, you know. I've pointed out the disease. The remedy is up to you."

"I'll investigate this," I said. "I'll report my findings to you if you wish."

"Indeed I wish. I'll come back again in a day or so. I believe in the personal touch, sir," and with a grim "Good day, sir," he marched out.

I called in one of the older teachers in the school and told her the story and asked her to search the thing carefully. I wanted to make a thorough report to the man.

"We ought to get his energy and interest in the school if we can manage it," I added.

True to his word, he came back a few days later.

"Well, sir, what have you? Not forgotten all about it I hope?"

"No," I said. "I've not forgotten. I find that the boys concerned in the bottle fight were two groups of our boys who were dismissed after the main body of the school had gone home for the day and no teachers and monitors were on duty."

"Just what I said, nobody on the job, sir."

"And," I went on without heeding the interruption, "both groups of boys threw the bottles at each other without any thought of hurting anyone. They had no quarrel. It was just the reaction after the repression of the day, a very dangerous one, to be sure, but boys are heedless and thoughtless."

"Heedless and thoughtless—I should—"

"Another thing," I insisted, interrupting him, "I found that a few of these boys had taken milk from the neighbors' bottles to feed some stray cats they were keeping as pets in the vacant lot across the street from your home."

"Awful! Murderous weapons to beat the brains out of one another and then thievery! Just what I told you, sir. Now—"

I could restrain him no longer, and once more he pointed a solemn finger at me. "I demand of you, young man, that for the good of the children we parents have entrusted to your care, you search out these offenders and punish them, that you make every reasonable effort to see that the streets are safe places for the children of the neighborhood. My advice is to look for the leaders and the rest will be easy."

"I have one or two of them," I said.

"Good," he answered with a note of surprise.

"One of them is Henry."

"Henry? Henry who?"

"Why—your Henry."

"My son? Never, sir—you're joking, I'm serious in this. My son?"

"Well, suppose you ask him. He told me himself, and he keeps a couple of the cats."

Varying emotions chased themselves swiftly across the fine old face. Then a grin stole over it—

"Well, well, sir. I'm astonished: and Henry told you?"

"Yes—you see, there's very little a boy can do after school but get into mischief. In your day it was different. There were many things to keep you busy. Perhaps now, you could help us get some after-school activities for the children. Working together we could do something."

"I'll help you in any way I can, sir. This neighborhood must be a decent place for our children. Just show me how I can be of service and I'll be delighted to assist you." Then a vestige of the old grin appeared as he rose to go. "I believe in the personal touch, sir, the personal touch. I'll attend to Henry."

"This is one parent I can count on," I said as he walked out.

When the children needed a garden the teachers went to the real estate operator on the corner. He was interested at once and loaned us a nearby lot and allowed us a room in his office suite to store our tools.

He was one of the leaders whom we had made up our minds we should have. He was the kind to help make the school's needs the people's opportunities.

Fancy the busiest real estate man in our district allowing a troop of grubby young ones to prance in and out of his office daily for months, armed with rakes, hoes, spades, shovels, and trowels, to say nothing of the sheet-iron wheelbarrow that brought up the clattering rear.

This he did and smiled.

One day he was seated in conference with some dignified city officials whom he was trying to persuade to some civic betterment plan he had taken to his heart. The gardeners, hushed by the anxious teacher, pigeon-toed into the outer room. With unusual quiet, tools were stacked in the corner. Isaac and his beloved barrow came last. The children held their breath while he skillfully reversed his pet and leaned it against the wall. Alas—alack—the relieved teacher was taking the hushing finger from her lips and turning toward the door when that barrow slipped, slid, and the whole armory, each bit screeching its own note of protest, crashed to the floor.

"Bless my life," called the most dignified city official starting out of his chair.

Calm as a summer day, our friend merely turned his head and said, "Those kids certainly have the time of their little lives on that bit of land. I tell you, gentlemen, there's nothing like it. Back to the land! The land is the source of all wealth—All right, children," as they essayed to restore order out of the heap of hardware. "It's all right. Harry'll fix all that. The tools need cleaning up, anyway."

The streets and park in front of the school were bare of trees and we thought Arbor Day would be a fine time to plant some.

Accordingly a committee of teachers wrote the Park Commissioner asking for trees for Arbor Day. He wrote a very noncommittal note, the gist of which was that he didn't understand what children were going to do with valuable trees.

We were all discussing the note and wondering what next to do when the teacher came in from her gardening class.

"I think we have the trees. I met Robert Hull on my way in.

He's one of the Administration lawyers now, you know. I used to teach him. He wanted to know what I was doing with the 'kids and the spades' and I told him and mentioned our difficulty about the trees.

"'That's because you teachers are a lot of amateurs,' he said. 'You don't know how; the Park Commissioner doesn't know you from a hole in the ground; you don't cut any political ice and he doesn't know the kids' side of it. I'll go and explain to him and I have a hunch you'll get those trees.'"

We got them too—twelve beauties.

Each year after this a dozen trees were given the school by the park department. After the first year the trees were given, not because of individual requests, but because of the new relation established between the public school and the Department of Parks.

As the months passed people became as interesting to us as children. All sorts of folks with all sorts of stories came to school. The more we looked the more we found those that were most useful to us.

A motherly looking woman was shown in one day and stood looking at me as if doubtful whether she should come in or go out.

"Can I do anything for you?"

"Are you the principal?"

"Yes, can I help you?"

"I don't know, that's just why I came. I've been everywhere and don't know where else to go. I'm bothered my life out with a child. Not mine. If she was mine, I'd kill her."

"Does she come to this school?"

"Not a bit of it. She goes to no school and she's close on to twelve."

"Why doesn't she go to school?"

"No school would have her, I'm thinking, and small blame to them. She's one bad habit. She's a 'runner.'"

"A runner?"

"Yes, she's always going somewhere and never content when

she gets there till she gets somewhere else, d'ye understand?"
And she dabbed her perspiring face with a wadded handkerchief. Explanations were hard work.

"Well, she keeps our whole block on edge. We never know
what's to do next. But this last is the limit. Tuesday she walked
into my area where my baby was sleeping in its carriage and
lifted it and away with it down the block. She got tired of carrying it—he's a heavy child, and doesn't she go into another
woman's basement and take her baby carriage out and away she
pelts.

"To make a long story short, after we had called up the police
and the hospitals, she came walking up to me.

"'Are you looking for the baby?' she asks, meek as a lamb.

"'I am. Where is he?'

"'I left him down the street in Conlon's basement,' says she.

"There he was right enough. We went to the police lieutenant
and says he, 'You got the baby all right?'

"'Surely.'

"'And you got the carriage?'

"'To be sure.'

"'Well, spank the kid and close the case,' said he, and thought
it a good joke. Can you do something?"

I asked her to bring the mother of the little girl to see me.
They came very soon. The mother of the sinner was sweet-faced
and sad.

"I'm sorry Kate is so troublesome," she said. "She is very hard
to control. I cannot keep her in school. She runs out every
chance she gets and she is so trying the teacher is glad to have
her go. I have a crippled husband and I cannot leave him long at
a time so Kate is getting little or no training and she needs it."

The accusing mother listened intently.

"Hark you," said she as if inspired by a new idea. "If I bring
her here myself every day will you try to keep her?"

"I'll do my best," I answered.

"Then I'll do it," she said firmly.

Faithfully she kept her word. She escorted her charge to and from school regularly for almost a year. Then the child came without her.

But the self-appointed truant office had got a personal interest in the school and the children that she never lost.

We were getting hold.

These were the old residents. If we could get them interested and active then they might not all go away. Some might stay with us and help interest the newcomers, holding them to the neighborhood and the school.

After some time there was a group of neighbors who through personal service had a genuine interest in the school life. They talked about the school to their friends, they talked about the school to their children. Their children talked about the school to them. Many times the children were the means of bringing parents and teachers together.

"Mother, please come and see my teacher," said one of our youngest children. The mother came, leading the child to the teacher's classroom.

"Mother," the child whispered, "isn't she lovely? She is so pretty. She has lovely blue eyes and she smiles all the time."

Some of the parents invited the teachers to their homes and the teachers went. The teachers invited the parents to school and some of the parents came. Now and then the teacher was asked to the pupil's birthday party, to mother's anniversary, or to a feast day celebration.

In and out the web was woven. Here and there children, teachers, and parents became more intimate, more friendly. The school world that had been sufficient within itself opened up its doors; a little at first, but as the days passed more and more.

II

We saw that the way to reach people and keep their cooperation was to give them work. Having secured individual cooperation we began to work for group cooperation. We wanted the parents to come into the school as a collective force.

What was the best way to get at it? We held many teachers' meetings—formal and informal—trying to devise a scheme that would bring the great mass of parents in touch with the school.

We had been struggling to do this for a long time and had succeeded only in getting the parent who was already interested in school and school matters to work with us. The parent who needed us most and whose interest we most desired to arouse was still a stranger to us.

We decided on a course of meetings. We would do what the other schools were doing at their parents' meetings. We would have concerts; the appeal of music was universal. We would have popular lectures by specialists. We set to work.

The concert was the first thing attempted. We secured the use of the building, and the services of fine musicians. The little group of parents already our helpers promised to come early and take charge of the program.

The evening of the concert came. The doors were opened. Henry's father presided. The teachers scattered through the rooms ready to greet the parents and make them feel at home.

At eight o'clock fifteen parents who had been in the school many times before were assembled in the big room that held five hundred. At eight fifteen, twenty-seven people were present. Another dozen strolled in by eight thirty, when the concert began.

That night we held a conference at the school door. What was wrong? We had done everything we could think of to make the evening a great success and this was the result. There were no explanations, no excuses. We had failed. We went home pondering on the perversity of human nature.

We tried again. This time we had a lecture on "Pure Food," a subject that was being widely discussed throughout the city. Again we made our elaborate preparations and advertised the lecture well in advance. Nobody came but our own little group.

"I'm almost afraid to suggest what I have in mind because it is contrary to what we have been teaching, but 'desperate diseases,' you know," said one of our primary teachers. "I think the only way you can get the average father and mother to school is to invite them to see their own children perform. The parents are in the school only because their own children are here. Let's have the next meeting an entertainment given by the children. I think the folks will come then."

"But it will keep the children up late."

"I've thought of that. We'll keep the actors in classrooms. Immediately after they perform the teacher in charge can take them out of the building and send them home. We'll let the younger children get through first."

The teacher had the idea. The parents were interested in their own children first. That was the place to begin.

The school naturally divided into grade groups according to the age and the needs of the pupils. There were the kindergarten and the first-year children. There was the primary group and there was the upper-grade group.

The teachers in each of these groups held parents' meetings after school hours. The parents came to the classrooms and saw the children and the teacher at work for the last school hours of the day, and then when the children were dismissed the parents met the teachers in conference. Then the discussion was specific. Whether the problem was getting a lesson or cleaning teeth or the need of fresh air, it was directly applied to the children.

We began also to color our evening meetings with the performances of the children whose parents seemed further away from us. The parents began to come. When they came once they were apt to come again.

All this time, however, the teachers were doing the work. But we were gathering the forces, preparing the way for effective organization.

Having done these things it was again decided to hold a large meeting. We were going to try once more to get the mass feeling in sympathy with the school.

This meeting opened with an entertainment—a play in two acts, given by the children. The school orchestra furnished the music. At the end of the first act I spoke to the people who filled the hall.

"My friends," I said, "I have brought you here to enlist your collective help in the work of the school. Acting together as a moral force in the neighborhood you are more vital to the education of the children than is the school.

"You remember the story of the cactus plant, how once upon a time, the cactus was a fine flourishing plant with luscious fruit. Then there came a change over that part of the earth where the cactus grew. The mountains heaved and the wind shifted.

"The valley that was once rich became barren and the plants died. They all died but the cactus plant, which, in answer to the new needs that the changing earth brought, toughened its skin and grew needles all over its body.

"The winds came with their sandy blasts and the cactus plant withstood their attacks. It had become ugly, repellent, and the beasts of the field could not touch it.

"Thousands of years after, a man came by who took the cactus plant and put it in his garden.

"Here there were no hot sandy winds. There was moisture and soft breezes and wonderful soil to grow in. The cactus plant changed and became once more the thing it had been in the beginning, a fine plant with luscious fruit.

"So it is with your children. You are the soil and the wind and the light in which the child, your plant, grows. You are the environment, the compelling force which by its influence, can make the children fine children, or can make of them warped and twisted natures unfit to live with, unworthy to carry on the ideals of your souls.

"Even if we could take upon our shoulders all the responsibilities of the home and relieve you entirely it would not be good for you and for the children. The children need you. You cannot afford to have the teachers take over your responsibility.

"You must share the common burden. You must all work together to make the conditions of life under which the children are living such that they will grow up healthy, intelligent, sympathetic, appreciative of the ideals of school, appreciative of the ideals of family life, and of fine American citizenship."

More meetings followed this one. Like the others these meetings were managed mainly by the teachers. As long as the meetings remained in the teachers' hands they belonged to the teachers; they were large classes for parents where the teachers played the main part, and the parents give largely a listening co-operation. What the parents needed was an incentive. Their coming together enabled them to talk to each other about school problems. Before we knew it, group opinion began to center on children's needs, equipment, children's work, school continuity, and moral training.

At first a few had come protesting about the shifting of children. They had come as individuals. Then more of the old residents of the district, disturbed by the conditions of things in the school and in the neighborhood, came in twos and threes and made their objections. They felt that the fine old school from which they had been graduated had been offered an affront— had lost its standing and prestige—and that they must have this adjusted.

This they told me as I met them in and about the school, and I appreciated their point of view, which harmonized with my own in that I felt the loss of the older children to be a serious handicap to the younger ones.

Among them was a young lawyer whose father as well as himself had been graduated from the school.

"I think it was a mistake," said he; "I think the local board didn't realize the meaning of their action. I know them all pretty well. The secretary is a personal friend of mine. In fact I asked for his appointment. I'll go over with a few of the folks and talk it over with them."

I saw him again a few days later. He was bursting with wrath and indignation.

"Think of it," he stormed; "think of it! We went over and there they all sat about the big table. I started to talk and the gentleman at the head of the table held up his hand and said, 'Have you an appointment here tonight?'

"'No,' I said, 'I haven't, I just came in to speak to you about our top grades.'

"'Exactly. Won't you have the secretary of your organization write to our secretary'—Billie, mind you—'and ask for an appointment and we will be pleased to hear you when we can reach you on the calendar.' And there sat Billie and never opened his mouth."

"What did you do?"

"What could we do? They asked us whom we represented—they intimated we'd better go and get a reputation before we came before them again. And we're going to get it. We're going to organize an association and go back. That's what."

The school had already furnished the impetus. The few leaders, confident of their strength and sure of their position with relation to the school, called a meeting. They tried to get the schoolhouse but they were too impatient to wait until permission was granted. The real estate man offered them his corner store as freely as he had offered it to the grubby gardeners. The people came not on tiptoes but talking, gesticulating, protesting. And this was the beginning of the parents' organization.

III

The parents wanted frequent meetings. They were impatient to get to work to see things done. But the school law provided that only four meetings a year could be granted.

There is that in each one of us that makes us antagonistic to a new idea—to a new point of view. We have been happily pursuing our course and someone comes along and suggests that perhaps it has not been the best one in the world and maybe his is better.

Our first impulse is to brush him aside—bowl him over—get him out of the way, anything so we may be comfortable again.

But that won't do. Society won't permit it. We must listen

more or less patiently while he dins his story into our ears. We argue the matter with him, we protest loudly, vigorously, with much waving of arms and stamping of feet.

We end by acknowledging he has much right on his side and if he had only said that long ago we should have understood him at once and saved much valuable time.

When the parents therefore asked for frequent use of the building the school authorities objected.

"No, no," they said. "It isn't done. 'Twould be a bad precedent."

The association urged and persisted.

"Yes, we know, you're respectable, responsible citizens but you're going to open the building to the public. They'll mar the furniture and damage the building. You must remember the school was built for the children. We must protect their interests."

"But we are the parents of the children—" came the reminder.

"Yes, yes, we believe you to be perfectly fine people, but you'd better hire a hall. You might say things we would not like to stand for. We'll let you have the building four nights a year. That's very generous. We hope you won't abuse the privilege."

The association was not satisfied with this concession. However, they accepted these four meetings and when they wanted more—and they did—they went to the real estate store or to the candy shop around the corner.

Then they decided that what the school needed was direct representation in the local school board. No member of the local school board had a child attending our school! Small wonder they did not understand the parents' requests.

Neighborhood opinion supported the idea and soon the chairman of the executive committee was appointed on the local school board. That was a great step forward, a strong link between the school workers and the administration group.

The parents were granted the use of the building once a month during the school year simply because someone who knew was on hand to explain the need.

They looked forward to the monthly meetings when matters of vital interest to themselves and their children were discussed.

These points were always carefully selected by the executive committee months ahead. The speakers were secured and the details of the program well worked up so that the meeting proceeded with the precision and efficiency of fine organization.

The usual "order of business" was followed: the various committees made their reports, which were accepted or returned for further work as the cases demanded. New committees for new work were appointed, and then the audience settled back to hear the special topic of the evening.

The executive committee, not the teachers, planned a health meeting. It was one of the neighbors who gave the talk.

This doctor began by telling us that the public school with its thousands of children coming from all sorts of homes was apt to be a breeding place for all sorts of contagious and infectious diseases.

In simple language the doctor told the parents how to protect their children from the contagious or infectious diseases, how to recognize the first symptoms of them. His points were illustrated with slides, the best of their kind.

"Only by utmost care and vigilance," were his last words "exercised by the school people, the Board of Health, doctors and nurses—and above all and beyond all—by the parents, can the health, the lives even, of the children be safeguarded."

The idea of the meetings was always a direct application of general principles to the immediate problems. If we talked about art, it was the children's art, with the children's drawings before us. If we talked about play, it was our children's playground, our streets that were used. We made no attempt to bring in outsiders for general talks. Our work was specific and always had for its outcome something to do, a job, a concrete thing. So much begins and ends in talk. We wanted to get things done.

Naturally one expression of the group feeling was its relief work. The parents wanted to help the children, the neglected children, to attend and to profit by their school.

A standing committee was formed. Its work was to investigate cases of parental neglect, cases of need, cases of truancy. These were simple and direct. They could be attended to without much room for argument. There was usually sufficient information at hand to insure promptness in relief work.

Red-haired Pat, small and ill-kept, did not attend school. The notices sent home by the teacher were unanswered. If a teacher called there was no one at home.

The case of Pat in the hands of the parents became a simple matter. The neighbors knew that the father drank and was seldom home. He had no job. The mother went out to work but could not make enough for food and clothing. Pat needed clothes. He needed food. He needed medical care. Pat was clothed, fed, had his teeth fixed. He was kept at school and that was the end of the matter.

There were other children like Pat in the school, who, for want of proper food, were unable to go on with their work; there were children who, because they lacked proper clothing, could not attend school; there were children who, because proper medical care could not be given them, were handicapped in their progress.

Physical needs were not new to the people. The ways of meeting these needs were not new to them. What was new was the group meeting these needs because it was their business to help their neighbors. What was new was the conscious strength that came through united effort, the feeling of responsibility that made them answer, "Yes, I am my brother's keeper, because he is my brother."

"Help me," was as natural a demand as its answer, "I will."

The judgment of the group was one that could generally be trusted. They loaned money to a family where the father was sick. The landlord was about to dispossess the family, the storekeepers refused further credit. The relief committee loaned them money, the family returning it in small installments when times were better.

One of the members of the committee was a clever, grayhaired Yankee lawyer. He was very much averse to anything that looked like charity and he had been placed on the committee to act as a brake on their generosity.

"Have you inquired carefully into this case?" he would ask, balancing his eyeglasses on the end of his sharp forefinger. "Are you sure? So many cases in a week looks queer to me. Before acting on them I'd like to ask for further investigation."

"Further investigation! That's the Charity Bureau's cry and while they investigate the family starves to death. No, sir, I say no. Relieve first and investigate last," this from Henry's father, who was now leader of the group.

"Very well, but you'll get stung. Mark my words. You'll get stung!"

One family made repeated calls for help. Groceries, shoes, medicine, rent, until even the leader was a bit worried and made a more thorough investigation.

When the final report was presented to the committee it revealed that many parents had at some time or other, without the knowledge of the others, contributed money or food or clothes to these people: that two large charitable organizations in the city were contributing to the support of the family in mutual ignorance of the situation, and the crushing fact that the imposters owned valuable property.

For an instant there was tense silence and then the old lawyer jumped up—and pointing his forefingers at the leader shouted triumphantly—"Stung, by George. Stung! Didn't I tell you! Didn't I tell you! Stung!"

Everybody rocked with laughter, but an investigator was added to the committee's staff, forthwith.

To make this sort of people better understand what the committee was trying to do, it issued the following announcement: "Charity is not the primary object of the association. We are not here to make parents careless and dependent. Our object is to help children and this we try to do, though in helping them we bring pressure to bear upon the parents to help their own."

Truancy and relief were intimately related. When a case of chronic absence was given to the attendance officer and he reported "poverty," the committee's assistance in supplying clothing was often sufficient to cure truancy. Sometimes "jobs" had to be found for the working members of the family. This was done repeatedly.

Other cases of truancy were not so simple. It was no easy task to get the corner boot black, big, ponderous, fat, to come puffing into the school building, with a struggling, kicking, yelling youngster, "a regular truant" he had found on the street, secure in his arms.

Neither was it easy to get the janitress a block away to send her children. Only the persistent daily visits of a member of the committee, the one who brought in the "runner," could succeed here. The attendance officer, stunned by the number and variety of excuses, could make no headway, but this woman, convinced that the children must attend school, paid daily visits to this family.

Some days she did not go but called at the school or sent a messenger. In case her particular charges were not in attendance she immediately started out, got the children, and brought them to school. In the face of such persistence there was only one way out: the children had to come.

The object of the association was, as specifically stated, to cooperate with the school authorities, to come individually and collectively into contact with the school so that the highest influence of heredity and environment could be brought to bear upon the education of the children—in short, to direct the group consciousness upon the welfare of the children.

Soon there were requests for information as to the work of the association. The president of the association, our garden man, felt that here was a new idea.

"I sent out three hundred copies of this morning's paper. There was a fine account of our work. Have you seen it? My clerk was busy all day, cutting, folding, mailing.

"This is getting to be a big thing," he went on. "A parents' association in every school! That's a big idea. I have been thinking of it for some time. What do you think of making a statement of policies?"

"Splendid," I answered, encouraging his enthusiasm.

"A square deal for the children," he announced vehemently, "means more parents' associations, a federation of parents' associations, cooperation between teachers and parents, the best teachers for the elementary school and for the youngest children, the masses, more schools, and smaller classes."

I smiled as I recognized some óf my own pet theories.

The president appointed a committee to answer questions and to lend every assistance in their power to parents who desired to form a like association in their school.

We are all preachers by nature. We get an idea and at once believe it is the most important idea in the world. Then like true reformers we launch into the campaign.

The danger of an adult association, however, lies not in this pushing enthusiasm of its members. The real danger comes when the association grows into a static, fixed, unyielding thing, itself a system. Parents' associations in the city are not apt to be static. They are more apt to be fluid. They are with you one year and away the next. There is always a group coming in and a group going out. They are always making mistakes, the natural mistakes of beginners. Their work is a constant challenge to the intelligence and patience of the school. Dealing with parents in the interest of children has always seemed to me like handling a dynamic factor, one that puts power and soul into the hands of the teacher because it puts power and soul into the people. Socializing the school means humanizing the teacher.

IV

No matter how many people moved into the neighborhood, no matter how many tenements there were or how full, there was always the park. When the school was overwhelmed with children, we looked out on the park and said, "There is plenty of air

and sunshine, there are plenty of trees, and shade and grass."
When the streets overflowed there was the park to receive the
overflow. When the summer nights were unbearable there was
the park to sleep in. It was always there smiling in the sunshine—
inviting the weary crowd to come out and rest.

But behold, one morning a startled parent came into school
saying, "What do you think is afoot? They want to erect an armory in the park and use it as a drill ground. This must not be allowed. We need the park for ourselves and we don't want
amateur soldiers about. I shall ask that a meeting of the executive committee of the Parents' Association be called at once."

Two nights later the executive committee met at the president's house. The fact was brought out that a bill setting aside a
portion of the park for an armory had been introduced in the legislature and passed. Time was precious. The civic committee was
appointed with full power to act. A meeting of the whole association followed. Then came a campaign, petitions, protests. The
committee appeared before the mayor when the bill was presented for his approval, and, joining forces with other park
lovers, secured its veto.

Aside from saving the park as a playground for the children,
the group realized that their united strength could achieve results even in the face of powerful political interests.

Two years later there was a second attempt at invasion. One
morning a park attendant told a neighbor who was strolling by
that he had seen a surveyor about and that a surveyor about
meant a building. The neighbor was a member of the Executive
Committee of the Parents' Association. At once there was a call;
the school committee began to investigate. A startling discovery
was made. Plans had been drawn for a firehouse to be erected in
the park and the money appropriated; ground was about to be
broken. There remained but one small formality—the location
of the building on the part of the park commissioner. This time
the association was ready. This time there was a united neighborhood to appeal to and a People's Neighborhood House
through which to conduct a campaign.

There were public meetings in halls hired for the purpose. There were continued meetings at the school, the settlement house, the neighborhood dispensary.

Then the Parents' Association called into play—and it was to them—a group of young men, none of whom was more than twenty. These young men belonged to the school group. They were getting ready to take part in the group activity of the adults. Here was their opportunity. They helped at the open meetings. They circulated petitions. They organized groups of younger boys, who paraded through the streets singing, "The parks must be free, the parks must be free for the people."

Sam, their leader, short, chunky, aggressive, and deadly in earnest, wrote an impassioned letter to the mayor protesting against the threatened invasion and calling the city fathers to strict account for it. He read the letter to the club, who enthusiastically approved it and ordered it mailed forthwith.

Eagerly Sam watched the mails for the reply and when the envelope bearing the City Hall crest came, he tore it open fully expecting a thrilling response from the famous letter writer. He got it.

Across the top of Sam's own letter in the mayor's neat chirography was penciled, "Who but a madman heeds what a madman says?—W. J. G."

The shout of laughter that went up was full of joyful appreciation of the old gentleman's cleverness and the joke on Sam.

After many months the city authorities, the park commissioner, and the neighborhood agreed upon a compromise. The firehouse was put elsewhere.

Once more, aside from saving the park, the group realized that united strength could achieve results even in the face of powerful opposition.

V

"Tony did it," gasped an enraged voice. I looked up. Framed in the office door stood Mrs. Mason in a sorry state. Tony, in one of his tantrums, had vented his resentment in a more forceful way than usual. Calling names, throwing stones would not do. Tony had utilized the ammunition furnished by the pickle barrel—the pickled onion, the scaly, salty fish.

Mrs. Mason appeared reeking from the fray. Onion peels and fish scales, coated her usually immaculate gown and the odor of dill was strong upon her.

"Tony did it. I want you to punish Tony. He is a little terror. We are all in dread of him. Just now he charged into my shop, pointed a penny pistol in my face, and shouted at me, 'Money or your life!'

"When I started after him he grabbed two handfuls of candy, knocked over the paper stand so I nearly fell over it, and made out of the door.

"I chased him and he raced into Rachel's fish store and this is what he did to me.

"If I get him I'll spank the life out of him. His parents don't care. He gets most of his ideas from the movies. Something out to be done. Teach these boys manners. Nowadays children have no respect for older people."

Mrs. Mason sank into a chair and suddenly a ripple of laughter crossed her face and she said, "We've got to get after those movies."

Mrs. Mason was a member of the executive committee and for hours watched the bright lights of the moving-picture show opposite her home. She saw the children playing about under the lights. She saw them beg to be taken in. She saw them go in unescorted. She talked with the neighbors about the "movie show," about the mysterious, dark influences at work to undermine the children's characters.

When the matter finally came up for official investigation she had a good deal of information. Then followed an investigation of many picture houses in the borough and of all picture houses in the school district.

The committee visited these places afternoons and evenings. Then they detailed the violations of law to the association. The association decided to call a meeting of the managers of the moving-picture houses. They came resenting the call and yet were too cautious to stay away.

The parents who had looked up the law on picture houses explained the law and described the violations in each place that had been visited. They asked each manager to remedy the evils of presenting poor pictures, of badly lighted places, of allowing entrance to unescorted children, of crowding men and women and children without regard to fire laws.

Especially indignant was the father of two little boys, aged nine and seven, who had stayed away from school and had taken nickels from their mother's purse in order to go to the movie show.

The parents demanded protection against conditions that were demoralizing to the children.

One of the managers present said, "You can't close up my place. I don't care if you do take me to court; the most that can happen to me will be a fine. I can afford to pay a fine and make plenty of money besides."

The indignant father who had secured evidence against this man presented the case in court. The manager was fined fifty dollars.

A week later a second fine was imposed upon the same man. In two weeks his house had to close its doors. Not only had the owner been fined but bulletins had been issued announcing the fact. Public opinion emptied his house.

There was no more opposition to our demands. We were asked by the managers to visit and inspect their premises and their pictures and to make suggestions for the betterment of both.

The Parents' Association had become a power for good in the neighborhood. It had earned the confidence of the people.

5

The Neighborhood Idea Keeps on Growing

I

What the children needed was leadership and direction.

When my family came to New York, I lost the companionship of open fields, grass, trees, flowers, sheep, streams, dark castles on the mountainsides.

In their places were flats, dark stairs, and streets—paved streets with trucks and boys running wild, empty lots, waste heaps. My companionship with nature was lost.

What a change from the sunshine, the open fields, the folk stories, the friends, to this crowded city life! And yet what a wonderful place is a city. Here life is seething, moving, searching it knows not what—fellowship? Common ideals?

The children left to themselves wandered mystified, guessed, tried first this thing and then that, and failed. Few, very few, through some fortunate accident, carried the dreams of their fathers into their lives.

I wandered about with the rest of the children, doing what we saw the older boys doing. Too young to find work for ourselves, we imitated those who were experienced enough to turn to their own uses what the empty lots and paved streets offered.

We played with pennies until the older ones took them from us. We used bad language because the older ones used bad language. We smoked for the same reason. We took what was on the vendor's wagon because the older ones praised us for doing it. We fought with our fists because the older ones encouraged us.

The streets and the boys who owned the streets were our masters. They did the training. Our parents worried and wondered. They punished us when they caught us. We learned to deceive, to cheat, to lie, to fight.

Through all this there was never a word of school. School had nothing to do with living and we were busy living.

When we grew older we formed our own little club and held meetings in a corner of the cellar where no one could intrude. We built a theater in one of the cellar storerooms. We took boards from the buildings and made benches. We searched for discarded mats and carpets. We ripped the "thriller ads" off the fences and pasted them on the walls of our theater. We made a stage and a curtain and gave our plays. What we needed to satisfy our dramatic instincts was leadership and a clean place.

The cellar walls of an abandoned building made our playground. We stayed home from school and sailed planks on the water that had gathered between the decaying walls. We hopped from wall to wall, across openings, at the risk of life and limb. We fell into dirty water and made a fire to dry our clothes. We went home only when we felt we had to because we feared punishment. When we were late, we relied on our mothers to shield us. This was all bad for us, terribly bad. It was a life of chance with the chances all against us. What we needed to satisfy our play instincts was leadership and open spaces.

Where these cellars stood twenty-five years ago, there are rows upon rows of apartment houses, with stores and stables, and saloons and factories.

Many crimes have been committed in the spot where we played truant from school. It was bad for us twenty-five years ago. It is worse for the children of today, who must contend not against an indifferent, passive environment, but against an aggressive, sinful, depressing, fearful environment.

Many times I have heard people say that the children who had it in them to become good men and women would become good men and women, and children who had it in them to be bad would become bad. My experience has been different. I have seen perfectly fine boys go wrong through no fault of theirs. The school had driven them out and the home did not know what to do. I have seen beautiful natures with a passion for fine things become discouraged, perverted, lost, and through no fault of theirs. The home was powerless to help. The school did not understand.

What we needed as children was someone to show the way. Someone who knew us and valued us. Someone who would live with us and for us.

What we needed as children, children still need.

The teachers and I, conscious of the dangers that come to an active child from a random seeking to satisfy his desires, tried to make the people whose children were about us realize their responsibility while we ourselves did our share. We knew the children needed the older folk. We knew that we had only limited means of gathering and holding these young people together. All we had was the school and we were fast losing that except as a drill machine running eight hours a day during which time two schools in turn tried to master the prescribed book facts.

An eager little group of children waited at the door to speak to me as I left the school one afternoon. I recognized the leader in one of the school plays.

"Do you know," he began after an exchange of greetings; "do you know that the Dramatic Club can't meet anymore?"

"Yes," I said. "I'm very sorry about it."

"But what are we going to do?" and the anxious little faces pressed closer to me. "We've no place to go. We can't give it up," the little fellow pleaded.

"I don't know what we're going to do, son. The school is so crowded that we have to let two classes take turns in using a room so each room is used all day long. I'm trying to find some way out for you."

"We'll stay after school hours as we used to do."

"I don't think it would be right. You could not have a room until half-past four and it's too late then and the teachers are tired. When the other new school opens there will be more room and we can begin again."

The school, after all, narrowing down to routine, was such a faraway place, far away from the actual lives of people. How could we get close, so close to each other that we would be part of the people and they a part of us, and be "folksy" together?

A woman I knew of began by going into the crowded streets. She started in the spring, when the houses were emptied of the children and the streets were filled with their shouts, their games, their squabbles.

She arrived at the same time each afternoon. She began by going from one group of little mothers to another and helping them with their sewing. To some she loaned books, to others she told stories that were found in books. They boys were helped with their games. By and by there were excursions.

The summer came and passed. School opened and when these children returned they were a little different from what they had been. They were better, less selfish, cleaner, in spite of the vacation.

The cold weather came and it was evident that the street meetings would soon have to stop.

Nobody had any money. There was a stranded old house on the block. No one lived in it. No one wanted to live in it. The "Street Lady" called upon the owner and got the use of the house for the asking. There was no furniture, no heat, no lighting. But they began.

Bits of matting and cast-off carpets, chairs without backs, chairs without seats, anything that could be made of service, the children seized and carried to their house. Pictures, pictures out of magazines and newspapers, advertisements, moving-picture idols were cut out and were pasted on the walls.

An old stove was fed by the boys, who brought wood to heat the place. The library was a packing case. The books were just books, torn, dirty, dog-eared, battle-scarred by long and rough usage. But the books, the house, and all about it belonged to the children.

Could we build such a place where the boys and the girls would work together, plan together, live together, grow together?

We felt that it would be good for our children to have a house of their own to go to when they felt inclined. We felt that it would be good for the parents of the children to have a house that was different from a school because its atmosphere was of hospitality; where the seats were ordinary chairs that invited one to sit and relax; the rooms, ordinary rooms cluttered with delightful evidences of human occupancy; the people ordinary people who could chat about everyday things; the ways of living, the ordinary ways of living; and the doors opened because they couldn't find it in their hearts to stay shut.

Our personal interest in the adults was always secondary. We worked with them because we could get no results if we ignored them. Our primary interest was the child. What we sought was complete living for him.

The most popular meeting place for the parents had not been the school but the Hall. This was a great bare room in back of the candy shop, where we were welcome at any time—a most convenient arrangement when a meeting had to be called at short notice.

In the Hall we held our annual dinners. The food was cooked by the mothers in their own kitchens and taken to the Hall. The neighbors loaned the chairs for the diners. On these occasions the cellar was dressed up for a reception room and a very acceptable one it made.

It was a wonderful spirit that could work and hold a group of people together under such conditions. The people were big and strong and united. There was always the promise of bigger things to come. What change might the next day bring? When people are sacrificing, striving, they forget to think of themselves. They think of the idea only, and the idea marches on.

Many conferences were held in the Hall. We discussed again and again the need of a settlement. We needed leaders who would make it their business to live with the problems of the people, with the problems of the children. The only way to get these leaders was through the establishment of a settlement.

Our friends' sympathies were enlisted and through their generosity a settlement house was founded. The house selected was a mansion set on a big plot of grass with shade trees. The apartment houses towering on all sides of it had driven the owners away. They were glad to find a market for it.

Some repairs and alterations were necessary before the house could be used. Who was to take charge while the workmen were busy—and how could we use the lawn and shade trees at once for the little children?

We had overlooked my father. He had come into the school every now and then, looked about, stayed an hour or two, smiled, and gone home.

Now that there was work to do, he put his cot in one of the rooms, and had his meals sent in. To him the settlement, like the school, meant a place for children. As soon as he appeared, they gathered about him. Slowly, softly, he smiled and told them stories, and then more stories. He spoke in broken English, and in gestures, but the children understood. Again Crusaders marched; again the goblins grinned in unsuspected places in this house of dark rooms, plaster, paints, papers, windows, boards, packed furniture. Once more he was a soldier on his charger, and once more little children listened and adored.

At night, favored ones were allowed to come and stay with him. They came bringing their blankets. His one steady companion was a child on crutches who followed Father all about the lawn and the house. The two had long intimate talks and many, many laughs.

During the day the baby carriages rolled in over the lawn and under the shade of the trees, and the small boys actually hushed themselves that the baby brothers and sisters might sleep.

Early one day in that first summer the calm was broken by a voice shrieking: "It's fierce. Soup meat for twenty-two cents. How can poor people live?" It was Ruth's voice and a teacher hurried toward the rapidly growing knot of people about her. A flourish with a little stick toward the audience pointed the question.

"Sure, sure—that is right," they murmured. "And chicken! Full of sands their insides are and for that thirty-two cents. The thieves, the murderers, they'll starve us!" Fiercer plunges with the little stick and more assenting murmurs.

The crowd began to warm up. The teacher tried to edge closer to the speaker.

Now Ruth broke into Yiddish, still carrying the crowd with her, at the end of her sharp little stick and sharper little tongue.

Then in unmistakable English she called out, "Come, stand up, we'll break their windows, we'll—"

Now thoroughly alarmed, the teacher pushed close to Ruth. Immediately her face broke into smiles, "Ah, here's our school. They'll help us," and Ruth poured out her story.

"Bring your friends over to the House, Ruth, and we'll talk it over there."

Led by "the school" and Ruth, the group marched over to the House and the first of numerous meetings were held on the meat strike.

As time passed the clubs began to voice the need that the school had voiced so many times before: the need for play space.

Twice the school, its people, and its teachers had secured a temporary summer playground in the park opposite the school. Twice when the playground had been removed, they were disappointed. Then the settlement and the school decided that the time had come to secure a permanent playground. A conference was called at the settlement, to which the city officials came. A playground in front of the school was demanded. We wanted an organized playground conducted by a teacher, one who knew how to lead children to play.

We were all familiar with free play, absolute free play, digging about in ash heaps, pouring dirty water from one mud hole to another, fights, pulling the peddler's pack, baseball, where the older took what they needed from the younger. We wanted a supervised playground, where the various group activities were controlled by an idea and where sportsmanship and not force held sway.

Twice the school had tried and failed, twice it had succeeded only partially; now hand in hand with the settlement and a public-spirited park commissioner, we succeeded in securing a permanent playground for the use of the neighborhood children. We were all sure of a place at last where the boys who wanted to play could go and be free to shout, to compete, to win, to lose, to breathe deeply, and to drink in the sunshine and the wind.

The settlement, seeing as the school had seen that language difficulty was one cause of separation between parents and children, began the work of teaching mothers English. Each morning a group of mothers gathered in one of the club rooms. The babies were left in the game room in charge of a house leader, and the mothers laboriously prepared to go through simple English exercises.

Someday the school itself will bridge over the gap that exists between English-speaking children and non-English-speaking parents by helping the children to teach the parents in the school building itself and during school hours.

Each month ten thousand children, men, women of all ages, went in and out of the settlement house. Music, drawing, sewing, civic clubs, athletic clubs, literary clubs, occupied all the space there was. Michael and his mother were there. So were the Flannigans and their group. We looked upon the settlement as a moving, living force whose idea was one of service and not of power. Free from tradition, we felt that it would be the neighborhood social experimental station, finding out, working out, and then beginning again, never stopping long enough to standardize. We felt it would always be openhearted because it prided itself on the bigness of the new opportunities. Through it the people would be drawn together more closely and neighborhood idealism would result. It gave us the hope that someday the school itself would be a bigger thing than it had ever been before.

II

Many new children were admitted to the school in the spring. They came, they stayed till the cold weather, and then went away.

"This is a shifting population," said my friend the real estate man. "It's better than it was but it's still bad. They are beginning to settle, however. They don't change as much as they used to. Why, of the fifty-two flat houses I have charge of, twenty-eight were empty, completely empty, from October to May. When they come, they want a month's rent free. When they go, they forget to pay the last month's rent. I wish they would stop moving."

"So do I. Our changes of class registers are tremendous. Some years our transfer figures are larger than our register."

"They'll stop soon," he added. "They come up from the crowded East Side. They move up here for the summer season to get the air. In fall they have been in the habit of returning to their winter quarters. You see, there are two parks here and plenty of open lots. These folks can't afford to go to the country so they come here. A great many of them are sick, too. Go through the park in the morning and see the men and women on the benches. Some of them are tubercular; all of them need fresh air."

This then was the reason that the school kept the local doctors busy, that we were not satisfied with the little that the Board of Health doctor and nurse could do, and that we had begun to group our doctor friends into departments—nerve doctors, eye doctors, and the rest. This was the reason for the increase in our classes for atypical children, the anemic children, for groups of children with special defects, bad feet, bad speech, bad spines, bad eyes.

But what had this to do with us? We had been trained as teachers, not as doctors. Why should we use time and energy that should be given to the three R's, and allow children to rest, to sleep, to do special physical exercises in the school?

Whatever has to do with the growth of the child has to do with the teacher. No one can teach a sick child. It cannot be done. The building, the equipment, the books, the teacher, are all wasted on the sick child. A sound mind rarely dwells in a sick body.

The local doctors had been giving their services freely and gladly as the school needed them. They had been ahead of the parents in their service because their contribution was definite and could be made anytime they were called upon. But as there was no hospital near the school where the people could take their children for treatment, a great many times children's ailments were allowed to go unattended because the distance to the nearest hospital was too great.

The examination and care of abnormal children, always a difficult problem, had been a severe drain upon the school, because the institutions that could help were far from home. The teachers gave their afternoons and Saturdays to this work but even that was not sufficient.

I saw the doctors grouped, and the people helping, and I realized that the school was already building its hospital. What was needed was its concrete embodiment as an institution. The people and the doctors secured a charter from the state authorities and began work at once by opening a dispensary.

Shortly after the dispensary opened a Russian Jew presented himself at the office in school. He was very much afraid of intruding but he had something to say that had to be said, he explained, holding out a strong, white hand and smiling across at me with the kindliest brown eyes imaginable.

Wondering, I placed a chair and waited for his story. He laid aside his big soft hat and little black bag.

"You open a hospital, my friend?" he said. "I am a doctor. I would help."

I was about to explain that he must apply to the Board of Directors, but he checked me and went on.

"We are Russian doctors—me and my wife. We lived in a little town in Russia. Always we worked for the sick. No difference, Jew or Gentile. From morning till night, all night when they needed us, we worked for them. If they could pay it was good. If they could not, it was alike good.

"When we did not think of trouble it came. They rushed to kill us. Even the sick people we worked for—they came to kill us. I pushed my wife in the cellar, I fight, then I hide. See this scar on my hand—that I get from Russia.

"By and by we make our way to France, then to America.

America gave us a home, it gave us work. Now we want to pay back some little. We want to work for the sick children under the flag.

"In Russia I learned to cure the lame children. Show me some. I am a—how you say in English—a masseur doctor."

We set him to work and his energy and enthusiasm were wonderful.

One day he caught my arm as I passed his room in the dispensary. His face was transfigured, the tears shone in his eyes as he dragged me in.

"See, my friend, see, he walks. The little fellow, he walks again. I have made it so, I am like your Jesus Christ—I make him walk again, the little fellow. I am so happy."

III

Within three years after I had come to "My School," another school had opened its doors. But still we were all overcrowded. We demanded additional room. The classes increased in size and number. We asked for more schools and waited. But there was no relief. It was always in the coming. There were conferences, there were petitions, there were public meetings, there were local newspaper demands, there were letters aplenty, all dealing with the need for additional school accommodations. Temporary quarters were rented. But these were of little help. When the movement of population sets in a certain direction, there is no help; at least no ordinary help will do.

The president of the Parents' Association, who had been the most insistent person on school accommodations, headed a church committee and with the aid of our real estate man secured property on the northern edge of the school district and began a school building for which the people belonging to the church furnished the funds.

"I want you to go over the plans of the building with me," he told me one day as he came into the office with a roll of papers under his arm.

"There are to be sixteen classrooms, and an auditorium accommodating four hundred, with regular auditorium seats, not the desks we've had to use here. No more knee cramping, no more sitting doubled up when we hold our Parents' Association meetings. There will be a fine stage for dramatic work. In the cellar a large gymnasium is planned and the children can use the swimming pool. It is already in the building, marble, with filtered water. It is planned to have a roof playground in addition. The library is across the street. This will be a fine building. I have tried to put in it everything you have been telling us a school should have. There is room for shops, and a music room. It will be finished in two years."

"Those are fine plans," I said. "Your pastor is a first-rate architect. The whole thing is wonderful. We are a lucky neighborhood. Only yesterday the park commissioner gave us a plot for a garden in the park. It is located near the pond. And about four months ago a lady came and talked over the project of opening up a children's nursery. She has already secured a house not far from your proposed building."

IV

When the overlarge school recognized its social limitations and possibilities, it recognized also the need of a home visitor, a woman experienced in the ways of the world who knew things that a young teacher could not possibly know, who could grasp the neighborhood problems and handle them most effectively.

The Henry Street Nurses' Settlement had a branch in our district. Now and then the teachers had come across the nurses in their visits to the home. The teacher had gone to ask about a neglected child, the nurse, to see the child's sick mother. Many times the teacher and nurse worked together. When the school needed a home visitor because the teachers were too tired and the work become too heavy, the nurse suggested a woman "who had years of experience in meeting the people's problems."

Thus "Aunt Margaret" came to us. We begged money for her

salary. Those who gave it were our neighbors, the people with whom and for whom she would have to work.

The machinery of Aunt Margaret's department was simple. The human quality of it kept it and made it so. A little pasteboard box that suggested shoes and a little black bag that suggested efficiency were about all that was visible—and of course Aunt Margaret. In the black bag were the records of the cases for the day and a list of all the children's welfare agencies, addresses, and telephone calls, a street directory, a notebook and pencil, a handkerchief, a change purse, and some chocolate for children. All very simple and very human and most efficient.

The first day Aunt Margaret appeared a teacher came into the office looking very dejected. She had made a visit to the home of a child whose appearance indicated extreme neglect and the mother had ordered her out. The family lived in a basement. The teacher had knocked and entered. The mother met her silently. Her clothes were unsightly and the condition of the rooms was desperate. Scarcely anything was clean. The teacher at once had begun to explain to the parent that her child needed washing, needed clothes, and that a mother should not be so careless as to permit the child to go to school in such a disgraceful condition. Whereupon the parent had upbraided the teacher for coming to her house to find fault.

"You have no right," she had said, "to come here and talk about mine kid. Mind your own business. Teach mine kid and leave her clothes alone. What do you know about mine troubles, with your fur coat and your feathers in your hat? Go away."

And the teacher had come back to school and poured forth a tirade against home visits and against superiors that required home visits and against the school that encouraged such visits.

Aunt Margaret took up the story and the job.

"How do you do this morning? The teacher told me you weren't feeling very well, so I just ran over to see you. How's the little girl?" she asked. "Now don't disturb yourself. Sit right down on that chair. I'll get one for myself."

Before she knew what was happening to her the woman found herself in the most comfortable chair in the room and "Aunt Margaret" waiting upon her.

"My mother was ill a long time before I lost her and I learned how to make her more comfortable. She used to like to have me brush her hair. She said it rested her," Aunt Margaret chatted amiably. Her hands were already fumbling about among the sick woman's hairpins and during the brushing process the two became very confidential.

"Are you from the school?"

"Yes. I belong to it. The teacher told me you were sick," said Aunt Margaret.

"Such a fresh teacher! She comes in and says mine kid is dirty and I should shame myself. Mine God—I have such a sore on mine leg and mine arm that I can't move. I pull mine hair like crazy."

"But the teacher didn't know that," interposed the visitor.

"Sure she don't. Then for why she makes a face at mine kid and says she is too dirty to be by the other kids. She's got no sores nor no kids neither. Like a grand lady she is with her high heels and feathers and powder on her nose. Never she come here again, I quick slam the door in her face. The fresh thing!"

"Have you had the doctor?" asked Aunt Margaret.

"Yes, once I go by the doctor and he say, 'My dear woman, you must go to the hospital. You can't pay me for this job. It cost you a hundred dollars maybe.' How can I go to hospital? They will not take mine kid and the society will get her. Maybe I lose mine husband. He not come by me in hospital."

"I know a good doctor who will come and see you right here. He belongs to the school like me, and he will take care of you for nothing," and the deft fingers put in the last hairpin.

"Maybe he say for nothing and then charge me big money," and suspicion looked out of her eyes for an instant.

"No, he won't. He isn't like that. Now I'll get the little girl ready for school and I'll come back very soon with the doctor."

When the doctor came he said the "sores" were very bad.

"She must have a nurse here to dress these every day. She should really be in a hospital," he explained to the school visitor.

The woman cried out sharply—"No, no. I lose mine kid if I go by hospital. Maybe I die. No, I stay home."

Aunt Margaret asked the Nurses Settlement for help and one of the blue-gowned nurses called every day until the patient was cured.

In the meantime the little girl fell ill. Nothing we could do could save her. Neglect and poverty had weakened her so that when pneumonia attacked her she died. Aunt Margaret helped from first to last.

Some weeks later the mother came to school.

"I come to say good-bye," she said. "I go with mine husband in the country. But first I say good-bye to the school, mine friend, never I forget. So good you were, so kind. When I come back I come to see you, how you look. I wish you health—"

A few words of explanation was all that Aunt Margaret needed, for she was keen where children were concerned and knew what to do.

Were the children dirty? Somehow they were made clean. Were they hungry? Then they were fed. Were they brought before the children's court, Aunt Margaret was sure to be there to plead their cause. Was the father out of work? A job was dug up out of somewhere. One thought twice before getting into trouble, for while she helped you out, you got a stinging, blistering raking over when she had pulled you out.

Peter, one of the highlights in 4A, stole some pigeons. The indignant owner had him arrested and hauled to court.

Peter's father and Aunt Margaret appeared with him.

"I didn't steal 'em," said Peter, looking the judge straight in the eye—"I took 'em." Aunt Margaret gasped and the father made frantic gestures toward Peter.

"But they were not yours. What do you call stealing?"

"When I take it and I ain't got the right."

"Exactly. Now what right had you to those pigeons?"

"They eat my pigeons' feed. He never hardly feeds his and they come and eat my feed."

"Is that all you have to say, Peter?" and the judge's eyes searched Peter's face.

"And—a—I wanted the fantail."

"Exactly. Then you stole, Peter, and I ought to lock you up."

Peter hung his head.

Turning to Aunt Margaret, the judge said, "What kind of a boy is he in school?"

"He's a first-rate boy. We've never heard a word against him. His teacher says his lessons are very good. I think he made a mistake, your Honor. Perhaps you could give him another chance and we'll keep an eye on him. He's really a good boy."

Peter looked up gratefully.

"If I let you go home with your father and this lady this time," said the judge, "will you promise me not to take anything that isn't yours—even if you think you have a good excuse?"

"Sure—I mean—Yes, sir."

"Very well. Are you willing to take charge of him?" the judge said to Aunt Margaret. "You'll be responsible for him and if he does anything like this again you'll have to bring him back here to me."

"Yes, I'll take him," said Aunt Margaret, "and I'll see he doesn't come back."

On the way home Aunt Margaret took a hand at Peter.

"Look here—young man—stealing is stealing and there'll be none of it in your family. Do you understand? I'll take a look at those pigeons of yours every so often and if I find one there that I don't know about—I'll empty that coop—every last one of them will fly over your head. Mind that."

"I have more trouble," said my assistant to Aunt Margaret, "with ninety-nine, ninety-nine than with any other house in the district. It seems to me that anybody who is dirty, or sick, or a truant lives there. I wish it would disappear off the face of the earth," and the assistant slammed down a bundle of papers on her desk. "Every one of those slips stands for somebody in ninety-nine, ninety-nine—I wish I could find out what sort of a place that is."

Aunt Margaret reached for the slips and dropped them into her black bag, saying, "I'll look in today and tell you what I find."

Later in the day she stopped at the school to report.

"Well, I should say there was something wrong about that house. It's awful, I don't believe it's had a coat of paint since it was built. The fire escapes are jammed. The first-floor stairway looks like a dump. It's a wonder everybody in the house isn't sick. I've asked all the departments in sight for help, and they've all promised to get busy. The landlord says all he does is paint and paper but I don't believe it. I am going to make him show me.

"But I don't think we'll get very far at that. I went in to see Mary Ann's mother about her hair and what do you think she said? 'And what of that? Sure she has them. We all have them. It's a sign of good health.' Did you ever hear anything to equal that?"

"Lots," said the assistant. "Lots, I've heard a book since I began to get after ninety-nine, ninety-nine."

"Well, we'll see what the Board of Health and the Tenement Department will do for us," and Aunt Margaret gathered up her belongings and went home.

"How's ninety-nine, ninety-nine?" my assistant asked her a while later.

"Fine, we're a little cleaner. The children are looking better. I'm going around there this morning though to see Mary Ann. She isn't much better."

In a short time the school visitor returned. She was angry.

"If that place isn't the limit. I've just had it cleaned up and it's as bad as ever. I went in to see about Mary Ann and the minute I stepped into the hall I smelled something. I walked to the back and there under the stairs was a dirty old mattress and a heap of old rags and the smell of cats—I went hotfoot for the janitor.

"'What can I do?' he said. 'I told you you couldn't keep this place clean. It ain't my fault. I don't make the people. Now you see it for yourself. I got my troubles and they ain't yours. Yours ain't mine neither,' and he turned his back on me and started to walk off.

"'Who put that stuff there?' I demanded.

"'How should I know? I guess it was Rebecca's family.'

"I went right up and asked Rebecca's mother why she put that stuff out there and she said, 'I didn't put it there, the kids did.'

"'What did you let them do it for?'

"'I should let them do it? She asks me I should let the kids? They don't ask me. They put it there for a place for their cats.'

"'Their cats!' I exclaimed.

"'Sure, ain't they got any rights? The teacher of the Board of Health says they can't keep no cats in a house cause it ain't healthy. She says it makes sores on the baby, those cats. Then the kids put them in a place under the stairs. I ain't got anything to do by it.' She waved her arms overhead and shouted at me till I was deaf and dizzy." Aunt Margaret was out of breath.

"What did you do?" asked the assistant.

"I got the rubbish man to take the stuff out. Now I'm going to get rid of those cats."

She picked up the telephone and began talking.

"Yes, a lot of cats. Ninety-nine, ninety-nine. Catch them? No, I didn't. How can I catch them? Will you go up with your wagon and try? I'll catch what I can."

"Now, what do you think of that?" said Aunt Margaret as she hung up the receiver. "He says did I catch the cats?"

There were the dance halls and the moving-picture shows, always likely to become a serious menace to moral growth. To cope with the conditions, the school visitor had to stay in the district nights, Saturdays and Sundays. She had to find out exactly what went on, who the leaders were, what temptations were put before the children to attract and keep them, and then to act in accord with this information, appealing to the law, to welfare societies, and to the parents, individually and collectively.

Usually reports of this kind made to the group of parents

evoked more interest and enthusiasm than any other kind. The visitor's vigorous crusades always resulted in better conditions.

V

But somehow I already had the feeling that the very presence of Aunt Margaret, even though she belonged to the school and to the people, was ultimately tending toward keeping the people out of the school and the school out of the home. She was here, there, everywhere. The people met her in the streets, in the homes. The more efficient Aunt Margaret became, the more the parents relied on her and stayed home, the more the teachers stayed in the schoolhouse and relied on her. I had the same idea about the doctors, the settlement leaders, the civic club. I wondered if the price the school had to pay for efficiency was a loss of the personal element, the very thing we had worked hard to obtain.

The school had stood alone, an imposing structure; about it a tall iron-spiked fence with gates that opened and shut at the appointed hour. Scarcely a soul that was not a pupil, a teacher, or a school official had ventured through its gates. They had passed, repassed, looked up, wondered what might be going on inside, and then passed on thinking, "What handsome buildings our schoolhouses are!"

I had come and asked the people to stop. They had stopped. By ones and twos they had come through the gates. Then we had gone on together, parents and teachers, sharing the children's problems. We had worked individually and collectively to push the school out into the neighborhood. "My School" had become "Our School." The teachers' school had become the people's school.

Through its efforts to get the people as the background for the spiritual growth of the children the school had succeeded in starting the mass movement. And then what had happened? The energy of the mass had begun to divide itself almost at the very moment of its greatest unity. Each group had begun to interpret the idea of service in terms of its own experience. Each had begun to think, "Mine is the most important work."

Those that had helped to care for the sick developed the dispensary. They believed this was the great neighborhood need.

Those that had been talking about overcrowded school conditions built a school. They believed this was the great neighborhood need.

Those that wanted the inspiration of personal leadership formed a settlement. They believed this was the great neighborhood need.

Those that wanted the spread of knowledge on civic problems organized a forum. They believed this was the great neighborhood need.

We had thought our worries were over, and they were only beginning in a new way. I realized that the problem the school was now facing was one common to many schools. There was scarcely a congested school district in the city that had not its settlement, its library, its hospital, its park, its charitable organizations, its civic bodies. Would the school be equal to the task of keeping the social forces working together, the children always as the center of united effort?

There was no answer. And yet I knew that the school must accept the challenge or again stand alone while the crowd passed by its gates. The school that had started the mass movement and had watched it take its course would now have to regather the mass and start it off once more.

6

Our School

I

While the school was engaged in the process of getting the parent to feel the power that comes through united effort, what was the school doing within its own doors to reflect the larger freedom and the closer human touches of the world outside its doors? What was the reaction of all this upon the life of the school? Very slight, I confessed to myself. The classroom work went on very much in the same way. Why was this?

I went back to my own experiences as a teacher. Many times I had the feeling of bondage. I was just one in a great machine and as long as I stayed in my particular corner that was sufficient.

The days slipped by in a monotonous repetition of bells, marchings, piles of yellow paper that seemed to distribute themselves to the deadening chant "Write your name, class, and date at the head of the paper. . . . Skip a line. Begin one inch in from the left side! Monitors collect. . . . Mark time, march"—and the day was over.

This kind of work I had to do day in and day out. Going home nights I was weary. There is no bondage so deadly as that which prohibits intellectual liberty. Intellectual slavery was what school teaching had meant to me at that time. It should not mean that for these teachers if I could prevent it.

I looked for individual strength in the teacher and put that strength on the work where it would tell. I felt that the teacher would grow only when allowed to use her best talent on behalf of the children.

Teachers' hobbies was what "my school" needed. The anemic class was given to one type of teacher, the atypical class to another, the backward class to another, the posture cases to one group, the speech cases to another, the disciplinary cases to the Child's Interest Committee. What we did for the special children during schooltime we now tried to do for the normal children, but this had to be done after school hours and in the teacher's own time.

The lover of flowers organized the Nature Study walks, the lover of music organized the Choral Club, the literary groups became the editorial staff of the school paper and the Storytelling club. Teachers grouped themselves according to individual tastes and inclinations. There were committees on festivals, athletics, dancing, embroidery classes, art classes, manual training classes. The children selected the class they wanted to join and soon the school hummed with the sounds of these different afternoon "shops." But one must finish his day's allotment of the classroom work before he could relax in the shops.

I was going the rounds of the building late one afternoon, as was my habit. This was a long time after I had become principal. I passed the assembly room. It was full of groups of children and teachers. Some were rehearsing, some were talking, some were just looking on and smiling. In another room I found a group of boys and girls making paper hats. In another half a dozen were drawing, putting in color, motion, ideas, and each proud because the drawing belonged to him.

I went on. It was late. School as such had closed its doors long since. Yet here were half a dozen teachers and a hundred or more children working, laughing, growing together.

I went into another room. A teacher was sitting there with a group of children about her. They had papers all about them. Now and then they stopped to read one aloud and the teacher and the children would say, "Let's save that one. That's a real good story."

When they saw me standing near them they looked up.

"We are picking out the good ones that are to go into the school paper," and the teacher added, "See what Isaac has written."

THE WIND

Oh! How I'd like to be the wind! I'd scamper all over the world.

I'd blow so softly, that the buds would say, "Spring is coming. Let's put on our bonnets of bright colors."

If I were at sea I would whisper into the captain's ear, "Spring is coming."

Oh! Oh! I'd have a jolly time frolicking all the day long.

I went out of the room smiling, feeling that the children were getting a sense of values, a sense of joyousness, a sense of laughter with their product.

The regular classroom, however, with its fixed curriculum, seemed the hardest to reach. It seemed almost impossible to vitalize the curriculum by means of firsthand experiences or to push the classroom out into the world. There was no time for cultural values here. The classes were large, the percent standard high, and the time limited.

A geography teacher who dropped into the office one afternoon epitomized this situation.

He was short and chubby—the sort that never stands if he can sit and never sits up if he can lie down, and the more sofa pillows the better.

He slid down into a chair and when his hands had found their accustomed pockets and coins and keys he made his plaint.

"'Head' came in today. Gave me a 'suggestive outline' for a geography lesson.' Says it'll 'stimulate thought and imagination.' Make you dizzy. Wait 'n' I'll read it."

Searching about in his pocket, he drew out a notebook and read: "Michael Zunich's father is going to move his family to Wilkes-Barre next week. This family came from the mining district of Austria. They are going to the mining district of Pennsylvania. Get Michael to tell his experiences in the old country, his voyage to New York. Get class to see why his father is going to Pennsylvania rather than stay in New York. Go over the route from New York to Wilkes-Barre, the distance, the cost, the time. Compare the coal and iron industries of the two countries. Get Michael to promise to write to the class to answer the questions that he can't answer now."

"Sounds interesting," I ventured. "Did you try it out?"

He snuggled further down into his wide collar and comfortable pockets.

"I certainly did not. That class has to learn the stuff that'll pass exams. When they come up for promotion, will anybody ask them to follow Zunich's old man around the globe? They emphatically will not. Where's Wilkes-Barre? What's the principal industry? What railroad? Just like that. That's what they need. Well, I'm off. Had a long day. Good-bye."

Gently he eased himself out of his chair.

"Good-bye," I answered. "Thanks for showing me the outline. You know I rather like that notion?"

"Which?" and he stopped in the doorway. "Oh, the suggestive outline? Stimulate thought, et cetera. Sure, I'm going to give it. I'll take the time from the literature. 'Head's' a good fellow. Do it just to please her. Good-bye."

A line from my old history flashed into my thoughts: "Dense and impenetrable forests lay between him and the entrenched enemy."

The classrooms were too strongly entrenched. I must try to break through by a new route—the school assembly.

The strongest impression of an assembly exercise I had carried away from my attendance at public school was that of the principal, day after day, reading to the assembled group, a chapter at a time, the story of *Black Beauty*. He could read wonderfully well.

The children understood every word he said. He held us spell-bound as he read through the story.

It was the cumulative effect of this reading that impressed me. The rest of the exercises never touched me. They were pieced up of odds and ends,—a recitation, a song, a quotation, with no relation of one to the other.

I never recall them without chuckling over the funny side of one disastrous November morning. We took turns in furnishing the "entertainment." This gave us each about two weeks to prepare. The morning I speak of fell to 4B. The luckless teacher had forgotten to give out the quotations until the night before and then in a perfect panic distributed the three stanzas of "The Rainy Day" to three pupils, conjuring them by all they held dear to be ready to recite them in the assembly the next morning.

That morning it rained as thoroughly and completely as a November sky could rain when it was in earnest about it. The wind came in great gusts, sending the leaves and dead twigs up against the windowpanes, where they tapped as if eager to get in from the storm outside.

Few children came to school and the big assembly hall was scarcely one-third full. The children started bravely to sing "America," but their voices, echoing strangely, frightened them, and they trailed out miserably at the end.

The principal rose and with all his accustomed grace and art read from the Bible the story of the man who built a great gallows for his enemy and was himself hanged upon it.

"So they hanged Haman on the gallows he had prepared for Mordecai. Then was the king's wrath pacified." The sonorous voice rolled through the silent room. The children sat scared and motionless.

He sent a sweeping glance over the room and solemnly closed the great book. This was 4B's cue.

The first child rose in his place and in a thin, little piping voice announced—

"The day is cold and dark and dreary,"

Swish, swish came the rain on the windows tap, crack, and a twig rapped smartly against them:

"It rains—it rains"—

the piping voice stumbled, stopped, and the child sat down. The second child rose and began tremblingly,

"My life is cold and dark and dreary—"

His voice trailed away and the storm once again filled the silence. A merciful teacher signalled the boy to sit, and the third one rose and announced in a startlingly loud and commanding tone—

"Be still—"

The principal swung about in his direction and looked at him fiercely. That was fatal.

"Be still," again declared the boy, and ceased.

"You have said it, my son," boomed the principal. "We will omit the closing song."

Aside from the single exception of *Black Beauty*, I do not remember the school ever staying with a beautiful idea long enough to have it become part of the children's lives.

Now, our assembly work was going to be worth while. A special teachers' committee, therefore, planned the assembly exercises. Their attention was first centered on literature.

Most of the children came from homes where English was spoken either not at all, or very poorly. There were a few of English origin. If our children were to grow to love English literature they must come upon it in a more vital way than they could possibly meet it in classroom work. In the classroom there was always a tendency toward grammatical analysis. Even in the treatment of Mother Goose there is, in the classroom, the temptation to use the stories as a basis for word drills, and little else. We wanted appreciation, not symbols, and we were going to use the assembly as a means of getting this. We wanted to teach literature, on this occasion at least, so that it would become a permanent part of the child's life, and be carried home to his family, to his younger brothers and sisters.

We were gathered about the table viewing these points pro and con in the usual conservative tone of a teachers' meeting.

"I'd like to begin with a children's poet," I said in one of the pauses.

"Which one?" somebody put in.

"Longfellow," suggested the chubby geography man. "He's the easiest. 'Under the Spreading Chestnut Tree.'"

We smiled at his joke and waited for someone to make another suggestion. None coming, I said, "I thought about Stevenson. How would he do to begin with?"

"Splendid!" and a wiry little teacher who up until now had not uttered a syllable except to vote "aye" jumped to her feet. "He's the one for the children."

For the first time since we'd known her the Scotch burr had stuck to her tongue. Snatching up the book that lay near her hand she hurried on, a bright rose color appearing on either cheekbone and her dark eyes taking fire as she talked excitedly.

"Ah—he's a r-rare one I tell you. Here's the place we begin:

SINGING!

"Of speckled eggs the birdie sings
  And nests among the trees;
The sailor sings of ropes and things
  In ships upon the seas.

"The children sing in far Japan,
  The children sing in Spain;
The organ with the organ man
  Is singing in the rain.

"Do you get it? They're all singing—children all around the world in one great merry-go-round are joining hands and singing—that's the thing for you!

"Hark ye to this bit! 'Bring the comb and play upon it.' Can't you just see them stretching out their little legs and marching and singing—singing!

"Everywhere he starts them at it, the wind and the rain and the sea make music for them and away they go, dancing.

"And the pictures, they're wonderful. The wee yellow bird on the windowsill—the formless wind singing in the grass and the treetops—the tiny lad marching and singing in the land of pain—the wistful poetry of childhood—it's all there and so wonderful, wonderful!

"Man, we'll clap a glengarry and kilts on this old school. We'll stick a twig of heather in her hand and she'll march to Stevenson's music." She stopped breathless and glowing.

We chose Stevenson.

The Stevenson enthusiast never let up. She pointed out the best poem for the kindergarten, the best one for the 1A's. She recited one here to prove its music, another one in some other room to point out the nicety of its phrasing. She found musical settings for some and dramatic settings for others. She got some fine pictures that illustrated, in color, some of the children's favorites. So we recited and sang and marched to Stevenson's music until his spirit permeated the school.

On Fridays we had special Stevenson exercises in the assembly. We sang selected Stevenson songs, recited the last-learned poems; sometimes several children recited the same one, vying with each other to bring out its special beauties. I asked questions about the songs and pictures and poems and about the man who wrote them all and the children answered freely, joyously. At the end of the term all the children knew a few of the poems, while some of them knew a great many. Some two hundred children owned copies of the *Child's Garden of Verses*.

When we finished with Stevenson we went to Field and Riley. Then there were the Folktales that were handled in a similar fashion. Folktales, not scattered, but in terms of people: Russian, Irish, German, Norwegian, and Indian.

These were dramatized and the songs and dances introduced. We gave the children a sympathetic appreciation of people and taught them to take home these folk stories, tell them to their parents and get the parents to tell their own folktales. So would the children be kept close to their parents, giving and receiving values that were human.

The parents came to our Friday morning assemblies, sometimes a few, sometimes a great many, but those who came always smiled as they left and carried the spirit of the school beyond its doors.

When spring came I thought of the time of carnival in Italy, the huge masqued forms reaching to the upper windows of the low houses and the children pretending to be scared at their hugeness, running in and out from behind doors and corners. It was all a game that the men, women, and children played. Then there were the religious festivals, crowds, lights, processions, fireworks, color, laughter; a people at play.

The school needed a play day. I wanted the babies, the mothers, the grandfathers, the friends to feel, to think, to take their part in this thing for one day and so selected Arbor Day as our festival.

The school neighborhood soon got the habit of looking forward to Arbor Day. We knew it was coming when a month or more before the day the Dramatic Club began its work of selecting, of putting together, of changing, of rearranging the best scenes of the term's work in dramatics.

We knew Arbor Day had almost come when the duly delegated member of the Parents' Association reported that the Park Department had granted us twelve trees for Arbor Day, one for each grade.

We knew Arbor Day was very near when on Thursday the trees arrived, and the men came to dig the holes, and the school paper came from the press and we all went home praying for fair weather.

We knew it was Arbor Day when on Friday morning we woke

early and looked out to find a clear sky and a warm sun. We went to school an hour ahead of time just because we couldn't stay at home, or because we wanted to make sure that the final touch had been given to the building's decorations.

Before the doors were opened, there was an army of three thousand children, all dressed in their best, bright-colored and gay. With them were their mothers, their aunts, their cousins, and the babies in the baby carriages.

Those that could went to the assembly to see the play. Those that had no tickets of admission stayed in the streets and in the park waiting for the tree planting and the outdoor games.

A child announced the day's program. He was dressed as a herald and spoke through a trumpet. "Know all ye people that this is our Arbor Day. It is a special day of festivities for our school. It is our custom each year to plant twelve trees. At nine o'clock there will be performed before you the play of Robin Hood. At ten o'clock the tree planting begins. Each class plants its own tree. At one o'clock the school marches to the athletic field to engage in its sports. This is according to our custom so that one day in each year parents, teachers, and children may live together in the open. This is our Arbor Day."

Then away we marched to the park. The brown uniformed park men helped us plant the trees and when the 1A babies joined hands and sang and danced about their tree they beat time with their picks and shovels and laughed aloud in sympathy, and the big policemen in the background looked at one another and said almost wistfully, "We had nothing like this when we went to school. It's great to be a kid these days."

Then the games and the dances in the afternoon! The hurdy-gurdy men got wind of us and came smiling and chattering and grinding away and immediately all the little girls and boys joined hands and such a tumbling of little legs and flashing of bright-colored ribbons you never saw.

Beaming mammas and laughing teachers poured pennies into the hats, and the music and dancing went on. The boys played games, ran races, and proudly displayed their medals.

Then joy of all joys, the hokey-pokey man arrived:

"Hokey-Pokey—com' along,
Hokey-Pokey—no last-a-long!
Penny lump—
Penny lump."

When the long shadows began to darken the grass, we started home, with tousled hair and floating neckties, dusty shoes and sticky faces, and the memory of a great glad day.

II

What had become of the problem of school discipline, the friction that resulted when a teacher tried to teach and a child would not learn?

I had begun by punishing children that were reported, by all the means known to schoolmasters: detention, reprimand, lowered standing, suspension from work, parents' assistance, but following the child into the street and home had changed the point of view. The problem of making the child behave had become the problem of providing the best conditions of growth for him. The school discipline had given way to life discipline—and appreciation of social values, because the children that needed discipline needed the help of the community: the people, the teachers, the doctors.

Jacob was a very, very small boy when he first came to us. He stayed only a part of the morning the first day and did not come back for a year. Then he came for two hours more and disappeared again. Now Jacob was within the jurisdiction of the Compulsory Education Law. He had to attend school. Repeatedly therefore when the big man had gone out hunting boys, he had returned with this wee boy Jacob. In silence they would come through the front door, up the stairs, into the office of the primary department.

Then the big man would say, "Good morning—I have brought

in Jacob. He's small but he won't do anything. He won't stay home and he won't go to school. He is on parole now. If he does not attend we will put him in the truant school."

My assistant would look once more at Jacob, look severely, sharply, then in silence take his hand. In silence they would go down the hall. Jacob would be put in his class with fifty little boys, all sitting very stiff and looking at the teacher.

"Here he is again. Jacob, sit next to Joseph, and Joseph, be sure and watch him. See that he does not get away," ordered the teacher.

The seat was farthest away from the door. But somehow when the class least expected it Jacob would disappear. Usually he slid to the floor when the class was busy and wiggled his way over the well-oiled surface and out of the room. At nine years of age he had been in the truant school. And still when the big man went out hunting boys he came back with Jacob.

Then something happened. Jacob discovered a teacher he liked. She was teaching the first grade and a girls' class. Jacob was in the second grade, thanks to the truant school, but when he discovered Miss Katherine, instead of making his way out of the building he appeared dishevelled and dusty beside her.

"I want to be in your class."

"But," said the astonished Miss Katherine, "this is a girls' class and a first grade."

"Where will I sit?" asked Jacob.

Before the teacher could recover herself, Jacob had found an empty seat and taken it as if to say, "Let the world roll on, I'm happy."

The big man had lost his job. No matter how often Jacob was placed in his right class he found his way to Miss Katherine's room.

There was only one thing to do and that was to let him stay with her. Miss Katherine understood Jacob. He loved growth and the smell of growing things. He wanted to handle flowers, dirt, animals, and Miss Katherine saw that he got the chance. She understood what happened to Jacob on fine spring mornings when the roll was called and Jacob did not answer. She sent him on trips to his beloved woods and he brought back treasures of the outdoors. These he tended.

When he at last recognized that he had outgrown Miss Katherine's class he took his proper grade but reported daily to his first friend.

We were thankful Miss Katherine belonged to our school. While she took care of Jacob, the rest of us had grasped a new idea.

We made a point of assigning the troublesome child to a teacher whom he liked. The teacher-friend kept in touch with him as long as she could be useful. Sometimes the child outgrew one advisor and was assigned to another. Oftener the relationship lasted through his school life and beyond it.

It was this desire to help by getting strong influences to continue to be a part of a child's life that made us send the "Flannigans" to the settlement house.

When a parent came saying, "Please see that my boy behaves. He whips his little brother and throws dishes on the floor," the teacher gave the boy a parole card and the parent marked the home behavior and sent the card in to the teacher.

Josephine was troublesome. She was in the habit of coming in and out of school to suit herself. Her mother worked long hours and had no time to train Josephine. She did not want the child "put away."

"There's a woman nearby," said our school visitor, "who is lonesome for children. All hers have grown up and gone away. Let's ask her and see if she will mother Josephine."

Accordingly Josephine was transplanted. The new "mother" taught the child how to live for herself and other people, and sent her back home.

"I could teach," the teacher had said, "if someone would make them behave." Now she said, "Something is wrong with Jacob." Instead of thinking of Jacob merely as an interference, as a challenge to her ability to hold her position, she thought of Jacob as a little child crying out for her help. "He is mine to make behave" was becoming "He is mine to stand by and strengthen."

Sounds of voices in loud protest came from the end of the corridor and I went down to see what was wrong. Miss North was trying to talk to Mrs. Tavish and Mrs. Tavish was insisting upon doing the talking herself.

"But can't you understand me? I'm telling you I don't want him to learn. I'd rather he'd be stupid than dead," she shouted.

"He must learn. Harry must obey the rules of the school the same as every other child," firmly enunciated the teacher. "He's got to come to school every day and come early. And he's got to learn." Miss North didn't say this all at once. She said it as she got opportunity between the loud declamations of the contrary-minded Mrs. Tavish.

When I appeared there was an instant's lull and the panting teacher said, "I'm so glad you've come. Perhaps you can make Mrs. Tavish understand."

"Understand? It's me that understands. Haven't I been trying to make you understand the thing that's as plain as the nose on your face for the past two months?" and Mrs. Tavish's pleasant voice rose again in good-humored protest. I took her to the office and asked her what it was all about.

"It's about my Harry. Now I'm not standing up for Harry— and I'm not blaming him, either—nor the teacher—for there's them you can do with, and them you can't. It's the same with teachers as with children, you'll find."

"What did you want the teacher to do?" I queried.

"Just to leave the child alone. But she won't. She says she can't. I'm the mother of eleven, all alive and well, thank God, and Harry's the last, and if I must say it, he's a bit thick. As good a boy as ever stepped, but thick about his lessons.

"Well, sir, whatever got into that teacher two months ago she began fighting the child to learn his lessons. The more she kept at him the more she might, till she says, 'You'll have to stay in every night until you do every bit of your work.' True to her word, didn't she keep him every day till five and after?

"I didn't tell you that once Harry had the fits. He doesn't be troubled with them much unless his food goes wrong or something bothers him, but this steady driving brought them on. He'd come home from school and fall asleep at the table, then in the night he'd have a fit. The next morning he couldn't get up. He was all in. When he got ready I gave him his breakfast and started him to school. To be sure he was late but I thought 'Better late than not at all.'

"All this time I kept writing her notes and asking her to excuse Harry until one day she said, 'Bring me no more excuses. You must learn your lessons and you've got to come early every day.'

"She kept right on trying to make him learn and keeping him in every day until Harry came home and said, 'I won't go back to that teacher anymore.' Neither would he. I had to pull him out of bed and push him to the school door. I told her about it but, 'No, he must come and he must learn,' says she.

"'On your head be it,' says I and I just let the child sleep in the morning.

"And what next does she do, d'ye think?" and here Mrs. Tavish leaned over very confidentially and marked each word with her forefinger on the arm of her chair.

"She comes every morning before eight o'clock and she pushes my bell and says she, 'Is Harry ready? I'll take him with me,' till I'm so wrought up I hear that bell every morning before she gets on the block. Nothing I say takes effect on her. She just dunners and dunners away at the boy until he'll lose the bit of sense he has. She's got to stop it. Now, am I right or am I wrong?" and she leaned back in her chair with the patient air of one sorely tried.

"I think you're right. We'll have to let Harry alone."

"Good for you. I'm not blaming you for the teacher, I said and I say again, there's them you can do with and them you can't. And you must not blame me for Harry. Some we make priests, some we make stonemasons, and some we leave as God made them. That's Harry." She shook my hand heartily and went home.

I went back to the teacher and told her about the boy.

"Oh, I'm sorry. It's all my own fault. If I'd only listened. But I was so sure he was just lazy and I was trying so hard to cure him. Do you think I've hurt him much? Can't we put him in the Special?"

"That's the place for him," I agreed.

The Special was a very large, bright room. The children were selected for different reasons. Some were too fast and some were too slow for the measured work of the classroom. Some were unfitted by temperament or nerves for the pressure of the big group; each of them was an individual that for some reason or other could not go forward with the mass.

The equipment of the room was selected with the idea of liberty of action for individuals and groups. There were a few benches screwed in orderly lines to the floors; but scattered about the room were tables and chairs where children might group themselves for work. At one end a long rack of tools, lumber, and twists of reed and raffia stood ready for work. A sewing machine occupied one corner and a bookcase another. Pictures there were in plenty, with here and there a cast or a plant.

The teacher was a fine strong man who wanted to understand and help children. He could play ball, tell a story, tie up a sore finger, or give an arithmetic lesson with equal enthusiasm and appreciation, and he never lost his poise, not even when I sent him the "Five."

The "Five" were sturdy youngsters from the fourth and fifth years, a monitor-teasing, peddler-baiting, neighborhood-disturbing group—strong on ball games and street fights, the joy of the small boy and the bane of the teachers' lives. About the middle of the term their teachers discovered that they were going to be left back at the term-end unless some radical change took place. I sent the Five to the Special.

By and by I went in to see how they were doing. The teacher was busy teaching a group to add fractions; the remaining groups were disposed about the room. The Five were around a big table, very busy. "Corduroys" was in command of right and usage. "Put away the pads and take your readers," he ordered. "Now, Specks, begin. Go slow. The words I don't get will be counted a miss.

"But—"

"Begin, or you'll lose one for the argument."

They read around the table until the lesson was completed. Once they stopped to have an "argument."

"That *sur*-round the island," read Beef.

"That's wrong. It's sur-*round*—" corrected Corduroys.

"'Tis not. A minute ago you said *sur*-face, now you say sur-*round*. If it's *sur*-face then it's *sur*-round," Beef grinned in triumph.

For an instant Corduroys was held, then his face lighted.

"Get the dictionary, Specks."

"No, you don't. I don't know the dictionary. You ask teacher when it's our turn with him today. What he says I stand for."

"How are they getting on?" I asked the teacher.

"Great. I wouldn't ask any better. They take turns in teaching but they generally fall back to Corduroys. They'll more than make their grade. I wish you'd have Specks's eyes looked at, though. I think his glasses are not right. He gets very irritable after he uses his eyes for a time."

In the Ungraded Room were the children of defective minds. At one time these were our disciplinary cases: now they were our wards, to be studied and given every opportunity for growth.

One big overgrown boy had in the first months given us a great deal of trouble. As usual we appealed to his parents but they could do nothing for us. Morris was worse at home than he was at school. Schooltime came as a blessed relief to his mother. Then he was examined and put in the Ungraded class. Soon I missed him from the complaint list and went to see what he was doing that kept him out of mischief.

When I entered his room he was busy with a pile of stiff white paper, a brush, a pot of paint, and a stencil set. He leaned a card against the blackboard to dry. It read, "9 eggs 25 cents." "Teacher," he called out, "how do you spell bread?" Slowly the teacher spelled over the heads of three little girls she was help- ing thread big needles—b-r-e-a-d. With his tongue curling around the corners of his mouth, fingers tightly knotted about a very thick, bright yellow pencil, Morris printed each letter on a slip of paper. Then, assuming a very important bustling air, he began painting a card for "bread."

"What is it?" I whispered to the teacher.

"He's crazy to work in a grocery store," she answered. "He has a job for the afternoons. I've made the grocery shop the center of his work and it's surprising how he's getting on. He works his arithmetic on the grocery slips. He tries to read anything that has to do with the grocery business so I'm making a reader for him out of cuttings in this blank book," and the teacher pulled a long strand of raffia through a big needle. "He's just what you see him now all the time. For a day or so he was sulky and ugly but I saw him with the grocery slips and talked to him about them and he's been going ahead on that line ever since." Another strand was drawn through another big needle.

"Lucy's at her loom, you see. Usually she threads these nee- dles for the little ones but I don't want to bother her today. She has one of her fussy spells. When she's like that she can't do a thing with her academic work but she works beautifully at her loom. It's strange, but it seems to soothe and rest her. She'll work at it maybe all morning—then go to her table and do her lessons very nicely. We have an order for the rug she's making and that's a great help. When her mother found that the work had money value she wasn't so much worried about Lucy's spending time on it and stopped scolding her. She even sent us some rags for the rug. So that's settled.

"I am going to take Morris to the garden. He needs more physical work. I can tie it up to the grocery store and once he gets started, he will like it well enough to go on."

As I turned to leave the room, the teacher said, "It's story time. I wish you had time to tell us a story."

"Of course I have. I know a fine one."

Like magic the work disappeared into drawers and closets. Morris ran to the corner of the room, where a long roll leaned, swung it up the center of the room, and rolled it out, "the magic carpet." Every child sat down upon it and the story began.

I knew when I went away that the older ones would go on with their bench work and the littlest ones build a story of blocks on the magic rug. By and by the teacher would play softly on the piano and the little ones would sleep while the older ones went down to the gymnasium.

We had difficulty with the little foreigners who found their way to the school. It is so hard not to be able to make oneself understood, especially when one is little.

"Plis. I make finger, she no let foot." This from a tearful boy brought to me by a vexed teacher. The vexation vanished in a peal of laughter.

"Really," she gasped, "I can't do anything with him. He means he raised his hand and I wouldn't let him go out of the room. He doesn't know a word I say, and I don't understand him a bit. Just now I thought by his motions that he wanted to change his seat. I wouldn't let him and he ran out of the room. He didn't come back and I went to look for him and I found him standing in the hall weeping. I know now he was asking to leave the room but next time he'll try it a different way because I didn't understand this time, and I'll get it wrong again. Seriously, I'm wasting time, though. I have to stop for him so many times and the class must wait for me and lose part of each lesson."

We asked for the "C" or the Foreign Class for all such children. We had about thirty. The teacher assigned to the foreigners was an older teacher, one who had been a foreigner as I had been. Together we planned for these children. We compared notes and resolved that our difficulties should not be theirs. There should be plenty of toys, pictures, maps, stories, dramatics, games, action and color and music. And there should be no difficulty or misunderstanding about leaving the room.

✿   ✿   ✿

There was an ornamental balcony open to the sky and facing the park. The Board turned it into a room for us and here we put the anemic children.

At first they didn't like it. They wanted to do just what the other children did. But the teacher was "lovely"—they couldn't help loving her. She had rosy cheeks and shiny eyes and little wisps of curls that danced about and when she said, "I'm so glad you came," they couldn't help being glad of it themselves.

Then there were crackers and milk. A mother came in to serve it and the teacher said, "I'm so glad you came," and instantly there was a proud son of his mother helping give out the mugs and another one vowing inwardly that it should be his turn another day.

But the best was to come. Long chairs were drawn out and each child wrapped in a blanket lay very, very quiet, wondering what was to happen next. Teacher sat where everybody could see and hear and began to tell a story of creeping, creeping bunnies who were sleeping, sleeping, sleeping, and no one ever knew what happened to those bunnies for no matter how many times the story started it never got past the sleeping, sleeping part.

The children grew taller and heavier and rosier. The place of honor was accorded the pupil who had gained the greatest number of pounds during the week and the race was close.

At the end of the term we found their academic work was ahead of that of their former classmates. Some of these children who in their weakness had been a serious drag upon the classroom had done more than a term's work in the open air.

Time and again we found that the children with whom we failed, the bad children, were physically or mentally unprepared. They had adenoids or bad teeth or poor digestion or sluggish livers; their eyes were weak or their ears were dull; their nervous reactions were slowed up or overstimulated. They were in no condition to be taught what we wanted to teach them.

We had first examined and regrouped the most striking cases of failure. These proved to be the physically and mentally retarded children. Still we failed with a group in each class. We couldn't get the whole fifty to measure up. We called in the specialists and they examined and regrouped the stragglers. Those who showed eye defects had glasses fitted and these were tested monthly for a year.

The Speech Defects were searched out, classified and drilled daily by a speech expert.

So we struggled on. Every time a teacher reported a child as falling below the class standard, we examined and classified him anew with the idea that it was his duty to reach that standard and ours to help him to it. We did this in the spirit of service. We must help him to realize himself and our only medium was the course of study, the seat, the book, the teacher.

Out of the seeming confusion of the great school's activities— the children playing, studying, shouting; teachers chatting, gravely conferring with fathers and mothers, visiting, teaching, presiding at parents' meetings; fathers and mothers coming and going, praising, criticizing, helping—emerged the great idea of our school—Service.

Service based upon the appreciation of the best that was in all of us—parents and children, principal and teachers. The slow realization that we were, all of us, "just folks," struggling under the limitations of humanity, was teaching us toleration and generosity and sympathy for each other. If our bones ached with the toil of the day, we no longer nursed them in isolation. We talked over the day's happenings, laughed at the funny ones, and stored the others away as experience.

I met the Assistant Principal. She was coming from a visit to the regular classrooms, studying the records she had made in her notebook. She looked up as I neared her with a worry line between her eyes.

"What is it?" I asked.

"I've examined and classified and followed up the individual child and yet I go to the classroom and find the group that can't 'make it.' There's something missing in the classrooms." She snapped the rubber band on her notebook and the worry line grew deeper. "Do you know, I feel like the old woman in the children's story. 'And still she sat—and still she spun and still she sighed for—company.' Does one have to be feebleminded or crippled or bad before he gets a chance to do things? All we have is pencils and paper and textbooks. No tools, no garden—fifty to a class, 'nothing doing' for us normal citizens. We just sit and spin.

"You've tried to remove every obstacle in the way of the children's progress, yet we seem to get no further ahead. We aren't alive. Do you realize that the little children may talk aloud about half a minute every two hours? That's about all we can allow them. When are they going to learn to talk English? They move about only at the teacher's command and they soon learn to wait for it and when they reach the upper grades they have no self-direction whatever.

"We're not to blame. It's the size of our classes. Fifty to a teacher and two classes in a room. We're simply turning out more candidates for Specials instead of making the Specials useless. I'm disheartened," and she turned wearily toward the office.

"Yes," I said to myself, "that's as far as we've got. Picking up those that fall, and doing nothing to keep them from falling.

III

Six years passed. The school that once held a little more than two thousand children had grown again to almost four thousand. As more children came the classes had to double up in the use of classrooms.

Soon there was little place and little time for the afternoon activities. The classroom time now reduced from five to four hours was all too short to accomplish the curriculum work. One group of children came from 8:30 to 10:30 and from 12:30 to 2:30—another group came from 10:30 to 12:30 and from 2:30 to 4:30. Five times a day the gong rang—I heard its resonance from floor to floor, calling, calling to the children to move. Five times a day

I heard the measured rhythm of many, many feet. I saw the surge of sound, and color and motion, children going in, children going out, eyes front, hats off, tramp, tramp, tramp and then silence.

All the rooms in the building except those used by the special children had to be given up all day long to learning the three R's. There was no spot where the child in the regular grades could turn for freedom. The biggest part of the assembly work had to be omitted, because the rooms, cut off by rolling doors, had to be used for teaching the rudiments of learning. The registers in each of these normal classes was full to the seating capacity—fifty to a teacher. Those in the Specials were kept down to thirty.

"There's a group in the fifth grade that must be scattered," said my assistant. "I don't understand it, but every once in a while that happens. A group of difficult cases get into one class and what one overlooks the other remembers. We might scatter them through the classes—put some in morning time and some in the afternoon so that they'll be separated, and if that can't be done they should be assigned to a strong teacher next term. Even with all our sorting we get one of these classes now and then that will not learn. I am afraid thirty percent of this class will have to be left back. But even at that we'll promote ninety percent of the school. Pretty good, don't you think?"

"Very good indeed. How did it happen?"

She looked a bit astonished. "Why, we've worked like dogs to get it. I hoped for more but we can't seem to make it. Do what you will, there's always a group of holdovers. The teacher has too many children, too little time, and always a fear that she won't finish the term's work; that we will find fault, that the superintendent won't be pleased, or that her class will not be up to the standard of the other classes."

As she started to leave the office, I said, "I'm tremendously interested in the ninety percent we are going to promote. Do you feel that they've learned? Are they really taking in what we are teaching them?"

The assistant laughed. "You are always looking behind the scenes."

"Sometimes I've been afraid that the real thing wasn't there even when the children answered with seeming intelligence."

The next day I went into a first-grade class. It happened that my assistant was there looking on. The class was just about to begin the reading lesson. At a signal from the teacher seven little fellows sprang up and distributed the readers to their rows.

"Open to lesson six. It has a big six at the top and the duck picture," said the teacher. "Ready? First row, begin!"

The first row sprang up in a flash. Each child read one sentence. Sometimes it meant five words, sometimes eleven, rarely more. Row after row in quick succession read. No child hesitated: no child made a mistake until the last row was reached.

"The holdovers," whispered the assistant.

These children read slowly, pointing at each word and sometimes miscalling one.

I knew what was in the assistant's mind when she went to the board and printed a jingle using only words that had occurred in the reading lesson.

> The dog, the fox, the cat,
>   One day,
> Woke up,
>   And said,
>   "O, a rainy day.
> We are sad,
>   It's too bad,
>   We cannot play."
> But the duck said, "Luck, Luck,
>   This is my own day."

"Who can read my story?" she said.

A troubled silence followed.

"I make a different g," whispered the teacher.

"Fix it up if you think that will help?" said the assistant.

Still nobody volunteered to read the story.

"Think, children," urged the teacher. "You know those words."

Still sorrowful silence.

Again the teacher went to the rescue.

"What is this word?" laying a pointer tip on "dog."

"Dog," came the answer.

"Certainly. Now what's this one?"

"Fox!"

"To be sure. Now this one."

"Cat."

"Now read the first story."

"The dog, the fox, the cat—"

"See, they know it. But they want to do it my way."

"Ask a child to read the line about the duck," said the assistant.

The teacher called a bright-looking child to read.

"Study it, William."

She pointed to each word along the line and the little boy nodded vigorously toward her as he followed the pointer tip with his eyes and lips.

William pointed at each word with a little stabbing motion and jerked his body forward and back as he recognized each word and went on to the next. With a final stab at the period he straightened to attention and read—

"But the duck said, 'Quack, quack!'"

"The last word, William, look again," and the pointer tip guided his eyes to the right place.

William looked, first at the word and then at the teacher— then again at the word and read, not so confidently.

"But the duck said, 'quack, quack!'"

"Hands, children. What is that word?"

Several hands came up and one boy said, "Luck, luck."

"Why, William, I'm surprised. You should have known that."

"I know it," said William, "but the duck always said 'quack, quack,' before."

As we went out I said, "Do you really feel they are ninety percent efficient?"

It was the children's own vocabulary. They were familiar with
the animals in the story. It was grouped into short phrases. It had
the familiar phonic elements. It was a jingle. It told a story, yet the
children couldn't read it. The teacher had to show the way for
each step. Without her they were helpless. The duck must always say "quack, quack."

"I've tried that same thing a half-dozen times this term, but I
get nowhere," said the assistant wearily. "The teacher says, 'I am
coming up for a seventh year increase of salary. The superintendent only asks what is in the book. With fifty children in this
room it's all I can do to get the children to learn the grade words
and the sentences in the book.'

"And after all aren't we teachers just that way? Haven't we
been taught to be afraid from the very first day we came to the
Kindergarten class and the teachers said, 'On your toes. Not a
sound,' as we passed the principal's office? Haven't we been
trained to give perfect results? Haven't we been trained to fear
making a mistake, to fear the responsibility of working out our
own ideas? This is a school world and we always say 'quack,
quack,' because we have said it before, and it was right."

As promotion time drew nearer I thought more and more
about these children who were to be promoted or left back. We
had taken out of the regular grades the children that were weak,
so that the others could progress, and yet the average child was
not doing work that made him independent of the teacher.

IV

I lived only a short distance from the school. I had settled in the
neighborhood to get the feel of the school in a rather intimate
way. Looking out of my window morning or evening I could see
the school building towering over the trees. It was only a short
walk through the park and all the many hours I would otherwise

have spent in travel were saved for the school. It was so convenient being near the school. A neighbor could drop in any time. A
teacher now and then might stop in on his way home. A child or
a group of them was sure to appear on a holiday. It was not so difficult to go out of an evening and meet some of the people and
talk over the needs of the children.

We never grew tired of talking about the needs of the children. We said the same things over and over again and the oftener we said them the more we believed we were right.

I do not know how many times we talked over better opportunities for the children, more vital things to do in school or the
Parents' Association. Somewhere in the course of the conversation
someone was sure to explode. He would become wrought up at
the slow progress of things, at the apparent indifference of school
officials, and we would listen and laugh and plan the next move.

The walk across the park gave me a good start each day, and
brought me back refreshed at night. I watched the seasons coming and going in their slow, calm, measured way. The trees would
bud, flower, fruit, and sleep again. Progress here had its own
measured steps and when I became impatient at school progress
the trees would speak to me and I would smile and go on again.
Many times as I walked among them I would catch the smile and
the nod of a stranger who thought my smile was intended for him.

Sometimes I would run over in my mind the things we had
done to make the child's lot better. There were the clubs and the
music classes at the settlement house, the children's departments
at the dispensary, the garden, the playground, the dramatics, the
poets, the music, the tree planting, the special classes, the speech
training, the school visitor, the parents helping in the school, the
big, human friendliness of the whole mass—children, teachers,
and parents.

Then my mind unfailingly went to the classroom and the class
teacher and I tried to figure out what was happening there to
make for freedom and courage. "It isn't what you teach the children that counts," the old principal who loved schoolchildren
had told me. "They forget most of the knowledge given them.

What they need is the habit of free thinking and the spirit of work." How much thought was there in the classroom? How much independent work?

Nowhere did the children, save those of the handicapped classes, learn by personal experiences, nor did they act independently. The classrooms had not been built to permit that. The classes were crowded. The children had to move in class units and exactly on time. The clamor of the gong was insistent. How rude and how frequent were its interruptions. I felt the hurry to get the facts into the children's heads. I felt the tension in the child's body as he bent to the routine. I saw the teachers standing over all, talking, measuring, urging.

Here was "Our School" still in the grip of tradition, rules, records, and endless routine. "My School" was still a dream school.

But growth is a slow affair. At least—or at best, perhaps I should say—we teachers had touched the people. We had carried the school out of its four walls and the school had been touched by the breath of reality, humanity. Socializing the school had humanized it.

7

The Direction of the New Start

The schools will change for the better when their life is made basically different from what it has been.

They are pointed in the direction of the fundamentals of knowledge but working with the tools of the classicists. They have developed and developed until we find life on one side, that is outside the school, and learning on the other side, that is inside the school. Now the schools must be pointed so that life and the school become one.

To begin with, better school conditions must be provided for the youngest children. The first steps in child teaching must be sound. The primary years of school must be worthwhile. Unless the basic structure is real, soul satisfying, higher education will be halting and futile. The child is entitled to a fine start in his life's journey if he is to have a fair chance of carrying his head high and his shoulders straight.

He comes to school a distinct personality. He is joyous, spontaneous, natural, free—but from the first day, instead of watching, encouraging that personality, the school begins to suppress it and keeps up the process year in and year out. By and by we begin to search for the individuality that has been submerged. We make tempting offers to the student in the high school and in the college—we give him better teachers, better equipment, greater freedom, more leisure, smaller classes, direct experiences. We call upon him to stand out, to face the problems of life honestly, squarely; to be himself. How blind we are! First we kill and then we weep for that which we have slain.

We do not look upon the children as an important economic factor. Children are a problem to the parent and teacher but not to the race.

Do you raise pigs? The government is almost tearful in its solicitude for their health and welfare. The Agricultural Bureau sends you scientific data gathered at great pains and expense. But do you raise children? Ah. They are very expensive. And there are so many of them! One teacher to fifty is the best we can do for you. Teachers who are specialists in their profession? Oh, now really! You know we could never afford that. We must pay for high-priced teachers for the high schools and upper grades but for the little children—all you want is a pleasant personality that is able to teach the rudiments of learning. There's not much to do in those grades—just the rudiments, you know. There's no disciplining to do there, the children are so easily suppressed. It's only in the upper grades we have the trouble!

Stupid and topsy-turvy!

We need the scientist, the child specialist, the artist in the first year of school. We need few children to a teacher and plenty of space to move about in.

It's there the teacher should eagerly, anxiously, reverently, watch for the little spark of genius, of soul, of individuality, and so breathe the breath of life upon it that it can never again be crushed or repressed.

We must spend more money on elementary education if the money we now spend on higher education is to bring forth results that are commensurate with our national needs. We spend fifty dollars a year on the education of a child and ten times that amount on the education of a young college man.

We must keep the three R's, but they must change with the changing social needs. They must keep pace with the world, and in fact a little ahead of the practical world so that they will be dynamic. Constantly they must be in touch with the strong life currents about the child, the factory, the mill, the shop, the market, the store, the garden, the home.

The school must be enriched so that the child can experiment with actual things from the very first day he comes to school. Playrooms and games, animals and plants, wood and nails must take their place side by side with books and words.

Be it remembered, however, that a shop, a studio, a playroom, may become as formal, as dead, as antiquated, as rigid as any phase of the present book school, if these activities are developed by rule and applied to all children regardless of tastes or tendencies, in accordance with a fixed time schedule that has neither elbow room nor leisure.

Just as we have failed to throw out the useless in the book study so we may fail to throw out the useless in the new things to come, if we center attention on them rather than on the child.

The school must constantly ask, "What is the effect of my program on the soul-growth of the children? Why is it that my program does not reach all children? What can I do to keep in touch with ideas that are vigorous and young? What can I do to keep sane, human, far-seeing? How can I respect the child's prolonged infancy and keep him from facing the struggle of the labor market until he is mentally and physically fit? How can I translate efficiency, goodness, will training, citizenship, parental duty into child happiness?"

The child is the permanent factor. The expression of himself for the common good is his purpose in life. Service that is in harmony with the best instincts of his soul is the child's mission in life. Service always carries with it someone else. Talking, cooperation, fun, openness are part of its very being. It grows with the spirit of the crowd from which it derives hope, life, strength, emotion.

I call this expression of self for the common good the art instinct of the child and I say that art puts the soul into everything the child does, whether he sweeps a floor, washes a wall, draws a picture, writes a poem, sings a song. The things he makes, the poems he reads, the compositions he writes, the games he plays, the clay he molds—all these need the force of an idea that is inspiring because it has the forward pull of this social art.

To take the child out of the narrowness of the printed page and put his energy back into the narrowness of the furrow of the plow will not make for complete living. The substitution of direct experiences for indirect ones leads nowhere. Both are needed, work and analysis of work, study and the application of study and, through it all, sincere artistic expression in answer to the needs of each individual soul.

Change the school so its life is continuous. Change the school so that the child may grow by intimate contact with older children and the teachers, the ones who carry the responsibility. Change the school so that each child is individualized and not merged, so that the child has leisure to grow and a desire to grow in the right direction.

Change the school so that it will permit the children to act for themselves and less by rule, so that it is not the teacher who shows the way but the child, and the teacher follows his lead.

Change the school so that the external, imposed dogmatism of school discipline gives place to real discipline, morally strong, self-made, independent.

We are now at the beginning of newer and richer educational possibilities. Have we the courage to think of the youngest child first, and this time begin our changes, not in the college, the high school, the upper grades, but in the first six years of school? Have we the courage to offer these children opportunities for joyous, expressive work? Have we the courage to change our class education into democratic education?

II

The first thing to do then is to change the kind of school, making it rich, making it live. The second thing to do is to train the teacher differently.

If the conditions of school life are such that they warp the child's mental powers, then these same conditions warp the teacher's mental powers. If the school means arrested development for the child it means arrested development for the teacher.

What briefly is the history of the teacher's training?

At six she goes into a first-year grade to begin the serious task of preparing for life. She may be too weak physically, or too immature mentally to start the routine of regular classroom work, but she is six and that's the age to begin.

For eight years the child who is to be a teacher sits and memorizes and recites, receives good marks, and is promoted. Her ability to recite the allotted lessons, though no test of spiritual growth, of human sympathy, are sufficient for school progress.

Now the child that is to be a teacher is sent to high school. The same grind continues, the same standards are practiced. She sits, memorizes, receives good marks and is promoted.

From the first day she began as a child in the baby class the teacher learned to be silent. She learned to be impressed. She learned to yield to force. She got into the habit of relying on the mind of another, of believing in books and words rather than in actions. She got into the habit of being afraid to think, to act; she merely followed.

"Come, quick—eleven times twelve—think now, why don't you think!" said one teacher.

But what was the child to think about as she stood dejectedly at her seat, a harried look in her eye? As the teacher passed on to the next girl, the child said, "I must think, I must think—next time I'll know."

The class went to the gymnasium. In one corner were the wands to be used in the day's drill. At once she remembered, "I must think." She left the line and was about to take down the wands from the rack when the teacher saw her. Snap went the teacher's thumb and finger and her voice followed after:

"Come here. What are you doing there without permission?"

"Why, I thought—" the child began timidly.

"You thought! What right had you to think? I'll do the thinking for this class. Take your place. We'll have no more interruption from you."

And this was part of the teacher's training.

Next the child that is to be a teacher goes to training school. By this time she is almost a machine. She knows what to do. She continues to sit, to study books, to make recitations, to receive percent ratings, to be promoted. By and by this child that is to be a teacher is examined, placed upon an eligible list, and appointed to teach.

The child that is now a teacher enters the classroom, the history of her training fresh in her mind. She begins to teach the children in the way that she has learned. The supervisor enters her room and because of the children's ability to reproduce the facts of the curriculum says, "well done," and rates the teacher. The training is nearly complete.

Later on the teacher decides to go back to the university so as to obtain promotion, so that she herself may become a supervisor. When she enters the university what is done for her? At once she is put into a seat, and handed a book. The professor talks, talks, talks. She writes, writes, writes. Words, words, words! Examinations come and she returns these words to him. She is marked, rated, and passed. Now and then there is an exception. The teacher gets a new point of view. She goes back to the classroom. But before long the continuous monotony of teaching the same thing in the same way, at the same time, with the same results has its effect and she succumbs, dies spiritually, intellectually!—now the training is quite complete.

How can the training be changed so that a new type of teacher may evolve?

Is there any change that can be made in the elementary school itself? Is it possible to vitalize the school so that the child who is to be a teacher may from the beginning learn from contact with more vital experience than mere school book-learning affords?

If the older children are trained to assist in teaching the

younger ones, helping in the classrooms with the lessons, or leading the games in the yards, then even at the age when they enter the high school they know in a dim way whether teaching is the right "calling" for them.

Can the higher training include the direction of young children in club life, the participation in the work of settlements, the study of the home and street life?

Should the training school period include work in the hospital for children, so that the teacher may actually learn what the physical needs of the children are, and where to go for help?

Should practice work be preparation for more intensive study in the training school and not the finishing touch? Should the student take back to the training school studies of individual children, their economic conditions, their history, their physical condition, their tendencies, and the attempts she has made to solve the problems they presented?

Is it right to say that a knowledge of subject matter and ways of presenting it are only a minor part of the teacher's training? What controls methods of teaching? Subject matter or children?

The teacher must be trained in this larger way because the burden of making a better school rests on her. She has been massed, she must cease to be numbers and be One.

O Teacher, find your inspiration in your work! Find work that will keep you mentally fresh. You, above all, have need of work that will make you grow, and what you do for the sake of the children is the only work that gives you life. With neighbors, fathers, mothers, with children, good and bad, you must cast your lot and as a leader plan the future of the race. Do not go to books. There is more philosophy—big, broad, human philosophy—in the simple folklore of some of the poorest and most distressed people than there is in most of the books that you read. It is only when you keep in constant touch with humanity that you see the child, more important than the curriculum, than the school, than the percents, than promotions.

To know the child, to work so that he may grow, is a far bigger thing than anything else in the world. You sometimes refuse to have anything to do with the child that presents a problem. You cast him off, because you are school-trained, not life-trained. You put the problem up to somebody else. When you do that you are lost. This is your problem. Only touch with life conditions can help solve it.

Like the child, you have been so long in bondage, dominated, that you have lost your strength, you are fearful, you sometimes lack the courage of your convictions.

But there is nothing to fear.

Speak freely, experiment boldly. You are a greater artist than he who paints a picture, than he who carves a statue, than he who writes a book. Your product is that wonderful thing, human conduct! You are a creator! America looks to you for her greatness, her united voice, her bigness of race!

III

First we must change the life of the school, making school experience life experiences; second, we must change the teacher's training, making the teacher life-trained, instead of book-trained; third, we must break the deadening influence of a too strongly centralized system; we must individualize the schools rather than mass them.

But is it possible to create public schools each of which will possess its own individuality, each of which will be the ideal school of its community?

The educational reformer usually starts his reform by projecting an ideal school. He does this in answer to what he believes the best parent, usually the well-to-do parent, wants, for his children. The reformer starts by carefully selecting the factors that go to make up the life of the school. He builds the plant, selects the children and the teachers, and lays out the work to be done. He tries to make his school distinctive, the only one of its kind.

Can the system learn a lesson from the private school and the educational reformer?

What the school system needs to understand is that its

strength lies, not in the strength of the central organization, but in the strength of the individual school, not in making one school like another, but in making each school a distinct unit. The need of the system is the preservation of its units, so that each school can keep itself alive, wide awake, responsive to its people, easily adaptable, the best of its kind.

Before the school site is selected and before the plans are drawn for the building, the neighborhood in which the school is to be located should be studied, so that the physical equipment of the building will be in conformity with the needs of the neighborhood.

The neighborhood being regarded as a unit problem, the school should be put in the civic center of the neighborhood, where the settlement, the hospital, the church, the library and the playground are. When these are lacking, the school should make provision for at least some of them.

If the school is the most important unit in the whole educational system, the principal and his staff are the most important officials in the system. Principals and teachers should be placed in each school because these principals and teachers are best able to meet the problems of the school. The business of the system should then be to help those in direct touch with the school problems, offering plenty of opportunity for growth.

Each individual school needs unity of organization.

There are school buildings that are used for day schools, night schools, summer schools, music centers, recreation centers, lectures, play centers. All these activities are in one building. All the people come from the same district. All the problems that the varied activities serve are the common group problems. Yet for each activity there is a separate head, each independent of the other and each responsible to its own department head.

The mere physical use of the plant does not mean complete use, definite heading toward a desired end. What is necessary is to make all these activities responsible to one leader so that he may coordinate them, permit their interplay. We have all the features of a settlement but without a leader or without a council of leaders. The result is isolation in the very work where there is need of the utmost coordination. Instead of using the people as the focal point for developing school activities, the system imposes a curriculum that the people must follow.

It is only a school with a continuous life and a continuous responsibility that can keep in touch with the neighborhood and, if necessary, help to create a neighborhood machinery that will get the parents to work together.

The great school is one that preserves its life, dignifies it, holds itself responsible for the neighborhood, and compels the neighborhood to rise to its highest level.

Unless a school enters deeply into the lives of the people, that school will not enter deeply into the lives of the children or into the lives of the teachers. Unless the school is the great democratic socializing agency, it is nothing at all.

IV

First we must correct the fundamental mistake that schools were made only for the three R's; second, we must change the notion that teachers are trained by being cast in a mold; third, we must change the idea that one school is to be organized just like another; fourth, we must change the notion that the school is a cloistered institution by breaking down its walls and having it come into direct contact with people.

In one school I found a common ground of appreciation in a cooperative garden idea.

We chose two gardens; they were dirty, garbage-filled lots. On one a neighbor street-cleaner was our partner. He was responsible for the general care of the plot. With him worked children who lived in his neighborhood.

To the children, the man working in the soil was a far more important man than the one who was sweeping the streets. Father farmer was more dignified than Father street-cleaner. The school had dignified labor and the parent, keeping in contact with the child, had become more hopeful. The school was no longer apart from the worker, but at one with him. Somehow the idea that the soil was our common interest made us forget that the home and the school were different.

If it is good to have a garden where everybody can see the children at work, is it not equally as good to put clay rooms and woodworking rooms facing along the streets, even as the trades-men's shops are, so that the passerby may stop and watch the children at work?

People have faith in the school even though they do not know what goes on behind the school doors. Because they have faith they throw more and more of their own responsibility on the school and the school shoulders the burden. The process must be reversed.

The school must stop doing things for the people and get the people to do things for themselves by putting the work before them in such a way that they will be able to do it themselves. It is in this movement out of a cloistered environment into the common lives of people that the school must share, because it means enriched responsibility through a consciousness of social values.

The school must open its doors. It must reach out and spread itself, and come into direct contact with all its people. Each day the power of the school must be felt in some corner of the school district. It must work so that everybody sees its work and daily appraises that work. It must put the responsibility on the parent, not so much the individual parent as groups of parents, so that the individual acts or refrains from acting because the group consciousness is at his elbow and not in a distant school, or in an unknown law.

The school must follow the lead of the social agencies. What have these social agencies done? They have gone out of their build-ings, out of their offices, and worked where the work would tell.

What does the domestic science teacher of a settlement house do? She does not teach merely. She goes out to live with her neighbors—those that need her, helps rebuild the home, then goes on to the next.

What do the settlement nurses do? They go to the homes and help the people take care of their sick ones, thus relieving the hospitals. Home care under wise guidance takes the place of the institution.

What do parents do who have come through united effort to appreciate school problems? They go back to the home and compel the parent to give the child a fair chance, and they compel by helping. The neighborhood holds up the individual home.

See, too, how the playground tends to shift. From the park to the backyards of the tenements. The children play and the mothers need have no worry. Play, children's healthy play, not harmful haphazard experiences, is going back into the home.

Dr. Montessori has taken the kindergarten school, the nursery, into the homes, directly in touch with the parents. The school is going back to the home.

In the schoolyard, I saw an old woman, her shawl about her head. She was talking to a group of children in her own native tongue. She was telling them stories, folk stories treasured for many years out of her peasant life abroad. Her voice was soft, dreamy. Her eyes were far off. The storyteller had come to the school. The home had come to the school.

One morning when the school was gathered in the assembly hall, a young man seated himself at the piano and played out of the fullness of his larger experiences, played the songs of the masters. Now and then he stopped, explained, and went on. The artist parent was giving to the children the best that he had. The home had come into the school.

The school has already done many of these things in a blind unconscious way. The school must now directly and consciously organize its larger social life. It must go out of its doors, as it were. It must use the factory, the stores, the neighboring parks, the museums, not incidentally but fully and with deliberation.

The teacher must go to market with her children. She must take the drawing class to the woods, the lakes, the streets, the open yards. She must bring into the building the artist, the musician, the singer, the advertiser, the picture man, the storyteller.

What the schools need is the push of the crowd. What the crowd needs is the pull of the child life. The school must become the people.

As yet, the school has not been taken over by humanity. When the people recognize the possibilities of the school as they did those of the printing press, the school will become a thousand times more powerful in fostering race growth.

V

First, we must change the kind of experiences that are given in the school; second, we must change the teacher's training; third, we must individualize the school; fourth, we must give the school over to the people; fifth, we must change our attitude toward the child.

Do we really believe in children? Can we say with the Roman mother, "These are my jewels"? How long ago is it that the state legislature passed a bill enabling the canneries to employ children and women twelve hours a day? Fifty children to a teacher, adulterated foods, military discipline, are not beliefs in children. Enslaving mothers is not a belief in children.

Our belief in children, like our belief in many other good things, is mainly a word belief. What we need is a practical belief. We are still at the stage where we separate work and thought, action and theory, practice and ethics. If we would be saved we must follow the child's way of life. His way is the direct way. He learns from contact with the forces about him. He feels them, he sees them, he knows what they do to him. He thinks and does and discovers all in one continuous flow of energy.

The child says, "I am of things as they are. I am the fighter for the things that ought to be. I was the beginning of human progress and I am the progress of the world. I drive the world on. I invent, I achieve, I reform. About me is always the glory of mounting. I have no fear of falling, of slipping down, down. I have no fear of being lost. I am truth. I am reality and always I question chaos."

When the child begins to question the wisdom of the group, its religion, its literature, its dress, its tastes, its method of government, its standard of judgment, that moment the group should begin to take heed. It should take the child's questioning seriously. When the group fails to do this, it gives up its existence, it ceases to grow because it looks back, it worships tradition, it makes history in terms of the past rather than in terms of the future.

Belief in evolution is a belief in the child.

What the race needs is a principle of growth, spiritual growth that can never be denied. Such a principle it will find in the child, because the spirit of the child is the one factor of the group existence that in itself keeps changing, growing. The child is nature's newest experiment in her search for a better type and the race will be strong as it determines that the experiment shall be successful.

We develop national characteristics in accord with our adherence to a common ideal. We must therefore surrender ourselves for the common good and the common good to which we should surrender is epitomized in the child idea.

I feel that the attitude toward the school and the child is the ultimate attitude by which America is to be judged. Indeed, the distinctive contribution America is to make to the world's progress is not political, economical, or religious, but educational—the child our national strength, the school as the medium through which the adult is to be remade.

What an ideal for the American people!

When my father came to America he thought of America only as a temporary home. He learned little or no English. As the years went by he would say, "It is enough; my children know English." Then more years rolled by. One day he came to me and asked me to help him get his citizenship papers. He and I began reading history together. Month after month we worked, laboring, translating, questioning until the very day of his examination.

That day I hurried home from college to find a smiling, happy father. "Did you get them?" I asked.

"Yes, and the judge wanted to know how I knew the answers so well and I told him my son who goes to college taught me and the judge complimented me."

I have been a part of many movements to Americanize the foreigner, but I see that the child is the only one who can carry the message of democracy if the message is to be carried at all. If the child fails to make the connection between the ideals of the school and the fundamental beliefs of the people, there is none other to do it. The children are the chain that must bind people together.

I have told about parents growing because they sought growth for their children. I saw them grow through the initiative of the school. These were tenement dwellers. Would this thing hold where the parents are well-to-do, and the streets are clean and the music is of the best, and home ideals are of the highest and the social life of the neighborhood is intimate? Is it still necessary for the school to gather the parents about itself? Is it still necessary for the school to go out into the community and get the parents to consciously work as a group for the children's interest, to consciously shape their philosophy of life in conformity with the dynamic philosophy that childhood represents?

More necessary! If not to save the children, it should be done to save the parents.

No matter who the people are, they need the school as a humanizing force, so that they may feel the common interest, revive their visions, see the fulfilment of their dreams in terms of their children, so that they may be made young once more. Americanize the foreigner, nay, through the child let us fulfill our destiny and Americanize America.

8

The Children

Yesterday the rain fell and the snow. I bent my head to the wind and went on. Then I met a boy, a very small boy he was, not big enough to be at school. He ran to me and took my hand and smiled, and I laughed and raised my head and walked on, stepping lightly to the music of the rain and the snow.

Each day and every day, to school and from school, I meet you, hundreds of you. You smile and the welcome in your eyes is wonderful to see. You meet me and as you go you take me with you, free and joyous as yourself. Surely my life is blessed, blessed with the smiles of countless lips, blessed with the caress of countless greetings.

Do you feel that you have need of me? Know then, oh, my children, that I have far more need of you. The burdens of men are heavy and you make them light. The feet of men know not where to go and you show them the way. The souls of men are bound and you make them free. You, my beautiful people, are the dreams, the hopes, the meaning of the world. It is because of you that the world grows and grows in brotherly love.

I look a thousand years ahead and I see not men, ships, inventions, buildings, poems, but children, shouting happy children, and I keep my hand in yours and smiling dream of endless days.